ORGANIZATION AND OUTLINING

Instead of drilling students endlessly on . . . the super-
ficial aspects of writing (punctuation, spelling, and gram-
matical correctness), we should start early instilling in
them a rage for order which will habituate them to careful
planning and organization of everything they write.

"English—One World or Three?" Edwin W. Robbins

ORGANIZATION & OUTLINING:

How to Develop & Prepare Papers, Reports & Speeches

PRINCIPLES, PROCEDURES AND PATTERNS
OF ORGANIZATION AND OUTLINING
HOW TO ORGANIZE AND OUTLINE
FOR WRITING AND SPEECH

By J.F. Peirce

New York

H.L. Second Printing, 1977

Published by ARCO PUBLISHING COMPANY, INC.
219 Park Avenue South, New York, N.Y. 10003

Library of Congress Catalog Number 70-142254

Paperback: ISBN 0-668-02425-9

Library Binding: ISBN 0-668-02473-9

Printed in U.S.A.

To the Reader

This handbook on organization and outlining is an outgrowth of a course that I was asked to prepare for the Federal Systems Division of IBM, Houston, Texas. It was designed originally to teach engineers how to develop detailed outlines from which to dictate papers and reports. It has been redesigned to be of use to anyone (student, teacher, engineer, scientist, businessman, secretary, or clubwoman) who has a need to write carefully organized papers, letters, and reports or to give carefully developed speeches.

The value of this treatment of organization and outlining over other treatments of these subjects is its completeness. Whereas most discussions of organization and outlining describe no more than six to eight patterns of organization (and those briefly) and give only two or three examples at most, this handbook contains detailed discussions of twenty-two patterns of organization and one or more examples of each as well as cross references to related patterns and examples.

I hope that this handbook will find a place on your desk next to your other reference works and that it will be of frequent help to you in your writing and speaking.

J. F. PEIRCE

Texas A&M University
College Station, Texas

Contents

Illustrations

1

Organization and Outlining

The primary purpose of writing is to inform. Therefore, the test of whether your writing is good or bad is not so much a matter of how well it is written as it is of how well the reader can understand and use the information presented.

Clarity, then, is the most important quality of good writing. And clarity is largely a result of the organization that must of necessity precede all creative endeavor.

This organization is reflected in the outline of your paper. [*Paper* is used throughout this handbook as a generic term for all types of writing and speaking.] Thus, once you have outlined a projected piece of writing or a speech, it is a giant step toward completion.

The Relation of Organization to Outlining

Good writing starts at a carefully determined point and proceeds logically, step-by-step, to an announced destination (or conclusion), taking the reader along every step of the way. To do this, the piece of writing must have a systematic plan of development to help the reader follow your explanation and reasoning. This systematic plan is the outline.

While the outline cannot insure good writing, it can make writing easier and assure that what you write is logical, unified, and complete, that its parts are properly related and emphasized, and that it does not contain extraneous material.

At first glance, you may find it difficult to decide which comes first, the outline or its organization. The truth is that outlining and organization are one. The outline *is* its organization, and it is organization that gives the outline form and meaning. You must start with the outline (with putting ideas and information down on paper), and then, almost at once, you must begin to organize this information to give the outline form, or shape. And at the same time, you must develop the outline (its ideas and information) with explanation, examples, and proof.

But though outlining and organization are one, for purposes of discussion they must be taken up separately at times. Although this approach necessitates a certain amount of repetition, this repetition will help you to understand them and their relationship to each other more clearly and completely.

The Place of Organization and Outlining in the Writing Process

To outline effectively, you need to understand the overall writing process and the respective functions of organization and outlining in this process. Figure 1, following, is a brief summary of the writing process in outline form.

THE WRITING PROCESS

Thesis: The writing process consists of analyzing your subject, determining your reader, developing the subject through organization and outlining, writing a rough draft of your paper, revising it, and making a final copy in correct form.

1. Analyze your subject.
   1.1 Define the purpose and scope of your paper.
   1.2 Recall all that you know about the subject from your education and experience.
2. Determine your reader.
   2.1 Is he a technical or a lay reader?
   2.2 What does he know about the subject?
   2.3 What does he need to know?
   2.4 How can this information best be presented to him?
3. Decide on the preliminary development of the subject.
   3.1 Compose a title that defines or describes the subject to enable your reader to tell what it is about.
   3.2 Develop a thesis sentence that expands and qualifies the title to help you fix the subject clearly in your mind.
   3.3 Make a scratch outline that reflects your knowledge of the subject at the outset.
       3.31 Set your ideas and information down quickly.
       3.32 Check the relationship of these points, or headings.
       3.33 Arrange these headings in their logical or natural order.
4. For complex subjects, develop the scratch outline into a topic outline.
   4.1 Gather additional information.
       4.11 Search the library for available information.
           4.111 Make a working bibliography.
           4.112 Compile a list of authorities in the field.
           4.113 Read and take careful notes.

     4.12   Write letters to or interview the authorities in the field to secure information and opinions.

         4.121   Request permission to quote them.

         4.122   Include questionnaires for their convenience.

         4.123   Send them copies of what you write so that they can check it for accuracy.

     4.13   Do research and/or experimentation, taking notes.

   4.2   Incorporate this information into your outline.

5. For longer subjects, make a sentence outline.

   5.1   Gather additional information, as before, taking notes.

   5.2   Incorporate this information into your outline.

6. Using the final outline, write a rough draft of your paper.

   6.1   Write rapidly using a simple, straightforward style.

   6.2   Give necessary explanation, examples, and proof.

7. Revise the rough draft.

   7.1   Read through the manuscript quickly.

     7.11   Evaluate its contents, your approach to the subject, and the readability of your writing style.

     7.12   Make notes in the margins of needed changes.

   7.2   Reread the manuscript slowly, making corrections.

     7.21   Reorganize the manuscript if necessary.

     7.22   Add needed explanation, examples, and proof.

     7.23   Eliminate extraneous material.

     7.24   Polish your writing.

     7.25   Edit the manuscript.

         7.251   Check it for clarity and completeness.

         7.252   Check it for consistency of form and style.

8. Make a final clean copy in duplicate.

   8.1   Use prescribed manuscript form.

   8.2   Proofread the manuscript carefully.

9. Submit the manuscript to your superior or publisher.

Fig. 1, The Writing Process.

A Definition of Outlines

Outlines have been likened to road maps, blueprints, the human skeleton, the structure of a building, and the framework of a bridge. Such comparisons graphically illustrate what an outline is: a summary of a subject set down in abbreviated form (in a kind of shorthand). They also illustrate what an outline does: it guides you in the step-by-step development of the subject, visually presenting its form and progression.

An outline forces you to build your paper rather than let it accumulate as you write. It helps you to give the paper form, balance, direction, and purpose. And they, in turn, help you to express your ideas more clearly and effectively, so that your reader can better grasp and use them.

Although outlining is only a part of the writing process, it is an important part. It is the plan for writing, a list of the basic information to be discussed, and a visual check of the organization, emphasis, relationships, and completeness of the information. In the writing process, you merely flesh out the skeleton of the outline with additional explanation, examples, and proof.

Some writers, instead of beginning with an outline, prefer to set down everything they know about their subject without worrying about its form and then outline what they have written to enable them to put the information in order when they revise their manuscript. Which of these approaches you use is largely a matter of personal preference. The outline will serve the same purposes whether it is made before or after you begin to write. Figure 2, following, illustrates the value of outlines.

THE VALUE OF OUTLINES

Thesis: A detailed outline will make writing easier and insure that it is logical, unified, and
     properly emphasized.
  I. An outline can make writing easier.
    A. It insures that your thinking has been done and that all information has been gathered before you begin to write.
    B. You can write without interruption as a result.
 II. An outline offers a logical, step-by-step method of writing.
    A. It lists information in the order in which it will be used or presented.
    B. It illustrates graphically the form and progression of the projected paper.
      1. It serves as a guide during writing.
      2. It serves as a check of what has been written.
III. An outline insures that your writing will have unity.
    A. It allows you to check relationships between headings.
    B. It helps you to recognize and eliminate extraneous information.
    C. It enables you to see the gaps in your explanation and thinking and insert necessary information.
IV. An outline aids you in achieving proper emphasis in your writing.
    A. You can check whether ideas and information are arranged in the order that best reflects their relative importance.
      1. You can check whether points of equal importance are expressed in parallel grammatical form.

2. You can check whether minor points are properly subordinated.
  B. You can check whether your ideas and reasoning are clearly and completely developed with explanation, examples, and proof.
V. Therefore, a detailed outline will help you to produce a logical, unified, and properly emphasized paper [note that this statement repeats the thesis].

Fig. 2, The Value of Outlines.

Despite the obvious value of outlines, you should always keep in mind that outlining is a means to an end, not an end in itself. Slavish attention to so-called rules of outlining at the expense of your writing should be avoided.

Detailed vs. General Outlines

There is no more effective way to write (or rewrite) than to work from a detailed outline. A brief, general outline may be all that you need when writing a letter or other short work, but for longer works such an outline is usually insufficient. Even for a short work, the time spent preparing a detailed outline will be repaid with interest, for the more detailed an outline is, the easier your task of writing will be.

When you work from a general outline, most of your thinking remains to be done and much of your information remains to be gathered, and the constant need to stop to think or to gather information makes writing a slow and painful process. As a result, your paper may reflect the way in which it was written and be poorly developed and lacking in emphasis.

A detailed outline, on the other hand, reflects a greater knowledge of the subject than does a general outline. When you use a detailed outline from which to write, most of your thinking on the subject has already been done and most of the information has been gathered, interpreted, and related. Writing then becomes primarily a matter of developing your ideas with explanation, examples, and proof and of tying them together with necessary transition.

Outlines are not static. They are subject to constant change to reflect your increasing knowledge and developing (or changing) point of view with respect to your subject as you think about it and as you gather needed information.

The real worth of an outline is its sense of order and development and the information it contains that can be transferred directly from the outline to your paper.

2

Types of Outlines

Any piece of writing worthy of the name deserves an outline. How long and how detailed this outline should be depends upon the length and complexity of the subject, how soon the outline is to be used, and whether anyone else can be expected to use it.

In general, short works such as letters and memorandums require only a brief scratch outline; articles, essays, and short reports a detailed topic outline; and technical and scientific papers, long reports, and books a well-developed sentence outline.

The Scratch Outline

The best way to begin writing is to make a scratch outline to assist you in setting your information down quickly and easily. Since the scratch outline usually lists only the major points of a subject, it enables you to see the basic form and content of the projected paper at a glance.

For short papers, a scratch outline of from six to twelve points may be all that you need as an aid to writing. You can jot down a few points (facts or ideas) on a scrap of paper, number them in order, and be ready to write within minutes. But no matter how long or complex your subject, you should start with a scratch outline which you can develop gradually

The procedure for making a scratch outline

When making a scratch outline, try to capture your information on paper as quickly and completely as possible without slowing down the thinking process.

To do this, ask yourself questions about your subject, your reader, and your reasons for writing; then jot down your answers.

Figure 3, following, lists the basic steps in making a scratch outline.

THE STEPS IN MAKING A SCRATCH OUTLINE

1. Analyze the subject with your reader in mind.
   - 1.1 Recall all that you can about the subject from your education, observation, and experience.
   - 1.2 Set the points down as they come to you without worrying about their wording, punctuation, spelling, and grammar as you can make all necessary corrections later.
2. Check the resultant jumble of facts, points, and ideas to determine their relationships to each other.
   - 2.1 Eliminate extraneous information.
     - 2.11 Some points may be included twice in different words.
     - 2.12 Headings or parts of headings may contain information that does not apply directly to the subject.
   - 2.2 Combine closely related headings in complex sentences, in compound predicates, or in series.
   - 2.3 Divide headings that contain two or more points [such as this heading], and present their information in separate headings, or else subordinate part of the information [for example, *by presenting their information in separate headings or by subordinating part of the information*].
   - 2.4 Check for gaps in your information or reasoning.
     - 2.41 Supply the missing information if you know it.
     - 2.42 Make a list of needed information.
       - 2.421 Gather this information from reading, interviews, and experimentation.
       - 2.422 Incorporate this information into your outline.
3. Reword the headings, correcting mistakes in grammar, punctuation, and spelling.
4. Arrange the headings in order or number them to indicate their relationships [this is an example of an acceptable heading containing two points].
5. Recopy the outline (if necessary), so that you can use it more easily.

Fig. 3, The Steps in Making a Scratch Outline.

A scratch outline is informal by nature. Since only you will see and use it, you can use any combination of words, phrases, or clauses that will enable you to recall the information quickly. Once you are satisfied that it is in the best possible order and sufficiently complete, you can begin writing.

An example of a scratch outline

Figure 4, following, lists the notes I made while discussing the objectives of a course that I was asked to prepare for the Federal Systems Division of IBM, Houston, Texas, and how I amended them to form a scratch outline.

IBM COURSE NOTES

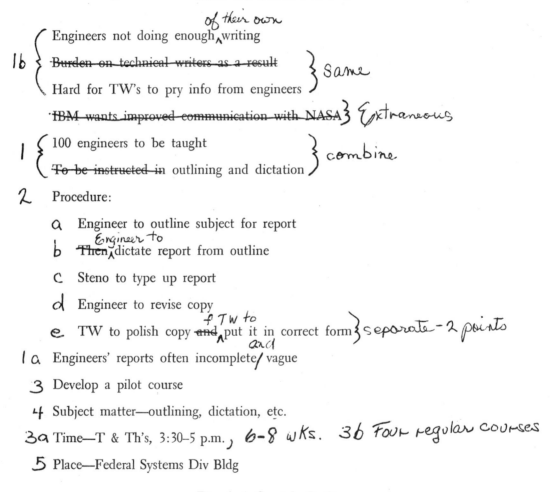

Fig. 4, A Scratch Outline.

Since a scratch outline can quickly lose all meaning for the writer because of its fragmentary nature, it should be developed into a topic outline if it is not to be used at once.

The Topic Outline

A topic outline is more specific and contains more information than does a scratch outline and is therefore easier to use, as its information can be incorporated directly into your writing without the constant need to stop to think or to obtain additional information.

The procedure for making a topic outline

To make a topic outline, you should do most of your thinking and gather most of your information on the subject before you begin to write.

Figure 5, following, lists the procedure for making a topic outline. This is largely an extension of the procedures for making a scratch outline [see Fig. 3, p. 17].

THE STEPS IN MAKING A TOPIC OUTLINE

1. Re-analyze the subject, keeping your reader in mind.
    1.1   Use your scratch outline as a guide.
    1.2   Ask yourself the following questions:
        1.21   Are there any gaps in my information and reasoning?
        1.22   Where can needed information be obtained?
        1.23   How can the subject best be developed?
2. Gather information from reading, interviews, and experimentation, taking detailed notes.
3. Incorporate this information into your outline.
4. Recheck the outline.
    4.1   Eliminate extraneous headings.
    4.2   Replace vague, general headings with specific information.
    4.3   Combine closely related headings by subordination or in a series.
    4.4   Divide headings that contain two or more points.
    4.5   Qualify (limit or develop) headings when necessary.
    4.6   Recheck for gaps in your information and reasoning.
        4.61   Gather additional information.
        4.62   Incorporate it into the outline.
5. Arrange the headings in their natural or logical order.
    5.1   Use numerals, letters, and indention or decimals and indention to indicate their relationships.
    5.2   Set them down in parallel grammatical form and wording.
6. Recopy the outline to make it easier to use.

Fig. 5, The Steps in Making a Topic Outline.

A topic outline is more formal than a scratch outline. Its thesis statement (if it has one) is the only complete sentence in the outline. The headings are words or phrases set down in parallel grammatical form (and at times in parallel wording) without end punctuation. Headings are set off visually with numerals, letters, and indention or with decimals and indention to show their relationships, whether superior (major headings), coordinate (equal headings), or inferior (subordinate headings).

While vague, general headings such as "Introduction" and "Conclusion" may serve to get you started in making an outline, do not fool yourself into thinking that you have said anything with such headings. Replace them with specific statements as soon as possible. You can often use the thesis statement as either an introductory or a concluding statement or both.

The degree of development necessary for a topic outline depends on whether it is the final outline or an intermediate step. If it is the final outline, you can begin writing once you are satisfied that your outline is complete.

An example of a topic outline

Figure 6, following, was developed from Figure 4, page 18. Comparison of the two outlines will show slight changes in wording, organization, and development as a result of additional analysis.

IBM COURSE PROPOSAL

Thesis: A course in outlining is to be taught to IBM personnel to get them to do more of their
        own writing.
  I. Problem
     A. To teach outlining and dictation to 100 engineers of the Federal Systems Division
        of IBM, Houston, Texas
        1. To get them to do more of their own writing
        2. To take part of the burden of writing off of the technical writers, who have diffi-
           culty obtaining information from the engineers
     B. To improve communication with NASA
 II. Solution
     A. To teach the engineers
        1. To develop detailed outlines
        2. To dictate their reports using these outlines
     B. To instruct stenographers how to type up these reports
     C. To teach engineers how to correct the typed copy
     D. To have the technical writers polish these manuscripts and put them in correct report
        form

III. Subject matter
    A. Organization and outlining (principles and procedures)
    B. Definition of terms (for clarity)
    C. Mechanics: grammar, punctuation, and spelling (for correctness)
    D. Dictation (principles and procedures)
    E. Editing (fundamentals)
IV. Course plan
    A. To set up a pilot course for twenty students
        1. Tuesdays and Thursdays, 3:30–5:00 p.m.
        2. Six to eight weeks (as needed)
        3. At the Federal Systems Division Building
    B. To then set up four regular courses of twenty students each based on this experience

Fig. 6, A Topic Outline.

The above topic outline was a sufficient plan for writing a short letter report describing the proposed course, but it had to be developed into a detailed sentence outline in preparing a course syllabus.

The Sentence Outline

To make a sentence outline, you need to do all of your thinking on the subject and gather all necessary information before you start to write.

The sentence outline is a summary of what is to be written. In effect, it is your paper in miniature. Thus you can often incorporate its information directly into your paper without changing a word.

The sentence outline is the most formal, specific, and completely developed as well as the easiest to use of the three types of outlines. It has the longest life expectancy, and remains meaningful and ready to use (both by you and by others) even after a considerable length of time.

Sentence outlines are primarily of use in writing books and long reports and in writing on complex subjects. Their use, however, need not be limited to these. They more than repay the effort they require, even when writing on the simplest subjects.

The procedure for making a sentence outline

The procedure for making a sentence outline is essentially an extension of that for making a topic outline [see Fig. 5, p. 19]. Figure 7, following, lists the steps in making a sentence outline.

THE STEPS IN MAKING A SENTENCE OUTLINE

1. Make a final analysis of your subject, using your topic outline as a guide.
2. Gather any needed additional information, taking careful notes.
3. Incorporate this information into the outline, as before.
4. Recheck the headings of the outline.
    4.1 Recheck and rearrange the order of the headings.
    4.2 Put them into complete sentences.
    4.3 Make them as specific as possible.
    4.4 Summarize information in closely related headings or combine them by subordination or in a series.
5. Recopy the outline to make it easier to use.

Fig. 7, The Steps in Making a Sentence Outline.

Since the sentence outline is, in effect, a summary, it may be shorter than the topic outline from which it is made. Related headings should be combined (through summarizing or subordination) in the sentence outline or set down in a series, as follows:

I. Types of outlines

A. Scratch

B. Topic

C. Sentence

I. The common types of outlines are scratch, topic, and sentence.

One of the major mistakes that writers often make when developing a topic outline into a sentence outline is that instead of writing one sentence combining a number of headings, as illustrated above, they may write four sentences—one for each heading. This is a waste of time and effort and can lead to wordiness in the final paper. Learn to summarize (to relate ideas and information), and making a sentence outline will become much easier.

An example of a sentence outline

Figure 8, following, is an example of a sentence outline that lists valuable information on note taking that should assist you when gathering information.

NOTE TAKING

Thesis: Good notes are an invaluable aid in outlining and writing.
  I. As an aid in outlining and writing, make careful notes when gathering information and performing experiments.
    A. Do not rely on your memory as it can play you false.
      1. Make notes of what you already know.
      2. Take notes on what you learn.
    B. For notes on your reading and on interviews, include quotations, facts, opinions, and brief summaries of information.
    C. For notes on your research, indicate where and when the research was performed, the materials and equipment used, and the results obtained.
 II. Paraphrase most of the information.
    A. Paraphrasing will increase your understanding of the information.
    B. The information can be incorporated into your writing more easily as a result.
    C. Set the information down clearly, completely, concisely, and concretely.
III. Use complete sentences when quoting or when your notes will *not* be used within a reasonable period of time.
    A. Quote when accuracy of phrasing is important.
    B. Quote when the authority's words will carry added weight.
    C. Quote when the language of the original is particularly colorful, descriptive, or forceful.
IV. Distinguish carefully between fact and opinion.
 V. Set your information and instructions down in a consistent form to make your notes easier to use.
    A. Make notes on 3″ × 5″ or 4″ × 6″ cards.
      1. Cards are easier to handle than paper.
      2. They hold up better with prolonged use.
      3. They are easier to file or to arrange in outline order.
    B. Give each card a subject heading (all in capitals, underlined; for example, NOTE TAKING) at the upper left to indicate the information it contains.
      1. Make separate cards with the same subject heading for each book, periodical, or other source used.
      2. File cards with the same subject heading together.
      3. File all cards alphabetically by subject heading while gathering information.
      4. Arrange them in outline order when you begin to write.
    C. Give the source of the information at the top right of the card.
      1. Give the author's surname and a short form of the title.
      2. List complete bibliographic information on separate cards, both for reference and for use in making a bibliography later.
    D. Give instructions for the card's use.
      1. Number cards on the same subject from the same source to show their sequence (for example, 1 of 3, 2 of 3, 3 of 3).

    2. At the left of the card, opposite the note, give the page number or inclusive page numbers on which the information is to be found.

    3. Print *OVER* at the bottom right of the card when continuing on the back.

    4. Print *MORE* at the bottom right of a card when continuing on another card.

VI. Systematic notes insure the accuracy of your information and save fruitless trips to the library to search for half-remembered information and quotations or for page numbers for footnotes.

Fig. 8, A Sentence Outline.

Other Types of Outlines

Though not directly related to the present discussion, two other types of outlines, the abstract and the paragraph outline, should perhaps be mentioned. They are more summaries than outlines and are made after a paper or report has been written, either by the author or by someone else (usually an editor).

Their purpose (or function) is to give the reader a quick, overall view, or preview, of the original, so that he can tell what it contains and whether or not he wishes to read it.

Like the sentence outline, they present the paper in miniature, but without the supporting evidence of the sentence outline. They differ from each other in that the paragraph outline summarizes every paragraph in the original, usually in separate sentences, whereas the abstract often summarizes several paragraphs in a single sentence and omits reference to those paragraphs that contain only examples or proof.

3

Outline Form and Evaluation

Conventional outline form permits you to set your ideas down quickly and clearly and to check the outline to determine how effective it is as a plan for writing.

Outline Form

Conventional outline form provides a pattern for setting your ideas down in sequence to indicate their order and relationships. It aids you in the step-by-step development of your subject and serves as a visual check, enabling you to see whether ideas are superior, coordinate, or inferior (of major, equal, or subordinate rank and importance) to one another.

The title

Display the title of your outline in capital letters, flush with the top margin, and centered with respect to the width of the page. If you need to display the title in two or more lines, divide it on the basis of its grammatical structure (before phrases and other sentence elements) and double space between the lines. For example, "The Use of Charts/in the Teaching of Propagation/at Texas A&M University,/ College Station, Texas," can be divided logically according to its grammatical structure at the points indicated by the diagonal lines. However, you would probably divide it as follows:

THE USE OF CHARTS IN THE TEACHING OF PROPAGATION

AT TEXAS A&M UNIVERSITY

COLLEGE STATION, TEXAS

25

Punctuate titles internally within a line [COLLEGE STATION, TEXAS], but unless the title is an exclamation or a question [WHICH WAY DEMOCRACY?], do not use punctuation at the end of lines. For example, there is no comma after *UNIVERSITY* or period after *TEXAS* in the title above.

The thesis

The thesis is located between the title and the first topic heading of the outline. Begin it flush with the left margin. It is usually labeled *Thesis* and followed by a colon. If the thesis requires two or more lines, double space [single space if there is a need to conserve space]. Indent the second line and all succeeding lines two-to-five spaces, as follows, depending on the numbering system used:

Thesis: Charts are an effective visual aid in teaching propagation, as they make the information presented in lectures easier to grasp and remember.

Numbering systems

Numbering is the use of numbers and letters in combination with spacing and indention to set topic headings off visually in an outline so that their relationships can be seen at a glance. The conventional numbering system alternates Roman numerals, capital letters, Arabic numerals, and lower case letters. Beyond this point, Arabic numerals and lower case letters are used and are set off by underscoring, l, a; parentheses, (l), (a); or some other indicator such as l', a'. The degree of development of the outline is dependent on the length and complexity of the subject.

In the fields of engineering, science, and business—decimal numbering systems are rapidly replacing the conventional system, and the decimals are commonly retained before their headings in the finished paper (or report) to provide a system of ready reference. In this system, pages are often numbered separately under each heading [1 of 1 pages or 1 of 3 pages, 2 of 3 pages, and 3 of 3 pages], so that catalogs, reports, and the like can be updated quickly whenever a part of the information becomes obsolete or new information is added. New pages with the same reference number and topic heading, but with a new date, are printed and distributed [1.1 Price List, 7/1/70, replaces 1.1 Price List, 7/1/69]. The old pages are removed from the loose-leaf binder containing the catalog (or report), and the new pages are inserted in their place, thus saving the time and expense of reproducing a completely new catalog (or report) every time part of it becomes outdated.

Figure 9 permits a comparison of the conventional numbering system with several decimal systems. All of the systems present problems. System 1 does not permit an even lefthand margin. This problem is solved in decimal systems by adding one or more zeros before initial digits if there are ten or more headings to a section [01.–10., or 001., 001.1–010., 010.1–100., 100.1]. If there are less than ten headings in any of the sections, the initial zero is normally omitted. Systems 2 and 4 do not always permit the alignment of decimal points and require too much horizontal space. System 3 can result in a duplication of numbers.

System 3 is recommended over the other decimal systems when none of the subsections of the outline have more than nine divisions.

NUMBERING SYSTEMS

[1]	[2]	[3]	[4]
I.	1.	1.	1.
A.	1-1.	1.1	1.1.
B.	1-2.	1.2	1.2.
II.	2.	2.	2.
A.	2-1.	2.1	2.1.
1.	2-1.1.	2.11	2.1.1.
2.	2-1.2.	2.12	2.1.2.
--	----	----	----
9.	2-1.9.	2.19	2.1.9.
10.	2-1.10.	2.20	2.1.10.
11.	2-2.11.	2.21	2.1.11.
B.	2-2.	2.2	2.2.
1.	2-2.1.	2.20	2.2.1.
2.	2-2.2.	2.21	2.2.2.
III.	3.	3.	3.
A.	3-1.	3.1	3.1.
1.	3-1.1.	3.11	3.1.1.
2.	3-1.2.	3.12	3.1.2.
B.	3-2.	3.2	3.2.

— Decimal points not on line.
+ Numbers repeated.

Fig. 9, A Comparison of Numbering Systems.

Indention and spacing

To be effective, indention and spacing in your outline should be orderly and consistent. Major points stand out only when minor points are properly indented to show their degree of subordination.

Begin superior topic headings flush with the left-hand margin, and indent inferior headings the proper number of spaces to indicate their degree of subordination. When the conventional numbering system is used, you will, of course, begin the Roman numeral requiring the most spaces [III if there are less than eight major headings, for example] flush with the left-hand margin, and indent other Roman numerals one or more spaces from the margin as necessary so that the periods will be aligned. Skip two spaces following the period before beginning the topic heading. Begin letters or numbers that set off subordinate headings directly under the preceeding larger heading.

I. Heading	I. Heading
II. Heading	A. Heading
III. Heading	1. Heading

When decimal systems are used, begin the numbers flush with the margin, using one or more zeros, if necessary, to insure alignment of the decimal points. Skip two spaces following the decimal point or if there is no decimal point, skip two spaces following the number before beginning the topic heading. Begin numbers for subordinate topic headings directly beneath the preceeding larger topic heading. When two digits follow the decimal point, skip only one space before the topic heading so that all topic headings will be aligned.

001.1 Heading	1. Heading	2-1.9. Heading
010.1 Heading	1.1 Heading	2-1.10. Heading
100.1 Heading	1.11 Heading	2-1.11. Heading

Triple space between the title and the thesis or the title and the first topic heading of the outline if there is no thesis. Double space between the thesis and the first topic heading if there is a thesis. Double space the thesis and all topic headings longer than one line. They can be single spaced if there is a need to conserve space.

Punctuation

Place a period or a decimal point after each number or letter in your outline [System 3, Figure 9, page 27, is an exception].

Align all periods and decimal points for like numbers and letters [Systems 2 and 4, Figure 9, page 27, are exceptions].

Do not use end punctuation for topic headings in topic outlines. If you do, you may be misled into thinking that they are complete statements. Punctuate topic headings in sentence outlines conventionally.

Capitalization

Capitalize the first letter of the first word of each topic heading and of all proper nouns in your outline. If you use the topic headings later as headings in your paper, capitalize them according to the conventions of the system of headings used [see the headings used in this handbook for examples].

Topic headings

Topic headings should be specific and make clear the information contained in each section of your outline. Superior headings usually summarize the information contained in a major section of the outline, and subordinate headings develop the superior headings with explanation, illustration, or proof presented in parallel grammatical structure and language that indicate their relationships to the other headings.

Subordination. When outlining, first divide your subject into major topics, then further divide it into subtopics (the degree of ultimate division being dependent on the complexity of your subject and how thoroughly you wish to develop it). This division of your subject into increasingly smaller units (or subordination) is the essence of outlining.

In subordination, you begin each section with a general statement (premise or conclusion) and develop it with increasingly specific details (description, examples, illustration, or proof).

Figure 10, following, illustrates the principle of subordination in outlining.

SUBORDINATION

I. Introduction—equal to V [Conclusion]
II. First major division—superior to A and B, equal to III and IV
    A. Explanation of or a significant fact that supports II—subordinate to II, equal to B, and superior to 1 and 2
        1. Source of A—subordinate to A, equal to 2
        2. An important point related to A—subordinate to A, equal to 1, and superior to a and b and $\underline{1}$ and $\underline{2}$
            a. Support for 2—subordinate to 2, equal to b
            b. Additional support for 2—subordinate to 2, equal to a, and superior to $\underline{1}$ and $\underline{2}$
                $\underline{1}$. Point related to b—subordinate to b, equal to $\underline{2}$
                $\underline{2}$. Second point related to b—subordinate to b and equal to $\underline{1}$
    B. Additional explanation of or a second significant fact that supports II, equal to A, and superior to 1 and 2
        1. Similar to 1 above
        2. Similar to 2 above
III. Second major division—similar to II
    A. Explanation or fact—similar to A above
        1. Similar to 1 above
        2. Similar to 2 above
    B. Explanation or fact—similar to B above
IV. Third major division—similar to II
    A. Explanation or fact—similar to A above
    B. Explanation or fact—similar to B above
V. Conclusion—equal to I [Introduction]

Fig. 10, An Example of Subordination.

Subordination helps to show relationships. If you give all of the points in your outline equal emphasis, then all of the points will seem equally important.

INCORRECT	CORRECT
1. Executive	1. Executive
2. Legislative	2. Legislative
3. Senate	2.1 Senate
4. House	2.2 House
5. Judiciary	3. Judiciary

Parallelism. Show that ideas of equal importance are equal by presenting them in parallel form in like grammatical constructions. Give them equal number or letter designations to show their parallelism.

INCORRECT	CORRECT
1. Executive	1. Executive
2. Legislative	2. Legislative [Congress]
2.1 Congress	2.1 Senate
2.2 Senate	2.2 House
2.3 House	3. Judiciary
3. Judiciary	

Items 1, 2, and 3 are of equal importance, but 2.1, 2.2, and 2.3 are not. *Congress* is equal to *Legislative* and superior to *Senate* and *House*. Therefore, *Congress* should be omitted or combined with *Legislative*.

In outlining, express parallel points in parallel grammatical constructions [all sentences or all phrases or all like parts of speech] and, when feasible, in like language.

INCORRECT

A. Offers a check of ideas

B. You can see the gaps in your thinking

C. Enables writer to recognize extraneous information and then eliminate it

CORRECT

A. You can check the relationship between your ideas.

B. You can see the gaps in your thinking and insert necessary explanation and transition.

C. You can recognize and eliminate extraneous information.

Don't force the use of similar language to achieve parallelism. Limit its use to major divisions of the outline and to individual sections of like number or letter. Since parallel language provides a pattern for increased clarity, clarity should be the basis for whether or not parallel language is used. Topics should be worded so that both their meaning and their relationship to other topics is immediately clear.

Breaking a topic down into its components is called division. If only one subheading is listed under a topic, obviously there is no division and therefore no parallelism. If you wish to list a single point so that you won't forget it, you can do so in the scratch outline, but in the final outline you should combine it with the preceding topic, either as a modifier or as a dependent clause.

INCORRECT	CORRECT
2. Legislative	2. Legislative
a. Senate	a. Senate, presided over
1. Vice President	by the Vice President
b. House	b. House, presided over
1. Speaker	by the Speaker

Figure 11 is a graphic illustration of parallelism, picturing the relation between numbers and letters of like order.

Outline Evaluation

The final step before you begin to write should be to evaluate your outline to determine whether it is an effective plan for writing. A close check of the outline will show whether it contains needless repetitions, omissions, faulty emphasis, poor subordination and parallelism, and so forth. This evaluation of the outline will help you to test the structure of your paper before it is written. It can also aid you in checking your paper after it has been written and found to be unsatisfactory for reasons that are not readily apparent.

You should insure that your outline has the proper tone, that the form and language of the outline are unobtrusive and do not distract you as you write.

You should also evaluate the proportions of the outline to insure that its sections are roughly equivalent (proportionately) to the amount of space that the information they contain will occupy in the completed paper.

One way to analyze the proportions of your outline is to make a dummy of the outline, putting down only the numbers and letters, as in Figure 11. This will enable you to see its overall shape and proportions without the distraction caused by the varying lengths of individual headings.

Another way to evaluate the proportions and content of your outline is to write a brief statement of the purpose (or function) of each example, opinion, statistical table, and the like to see if the outline is organically sound, that it does what you want it to.

PARALLELISM

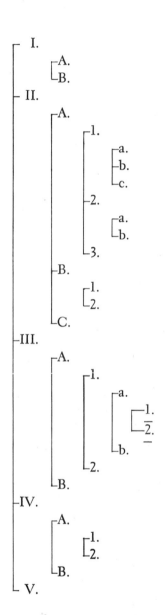

Each subsection within an outline is independent of every other subsection with respect to parallelism and arrangement.

You can use a dummy outline without headings (such as this) to test your outline to determine whether the proportions of its various sections are correct and to obtain a visual picture of the relationships of the various sections.

Fig. 11, An Example of Parallelism.

An example of evaluation

The commentary following Figure 12, "The Crusades," is an excellent example of outline evaluation.

THE CRUSADES

I. The causes
   A. Persecution of Christians and Jews
      1. Danger in travel
      2. Taxation of Jews
      3. Massacre of Jews
   B. Influence of clergy and Roman Catholic Church
      1. Desire for pilgrimages
      2. Desire for universal church
   C. Search for connections with East
      1. Famine and pestilence in West
      2. Riches in East
II. The wars
   A. The First Crusade
      1. The People's Crusade
         a. Leaders
            (1). Peter the Hermit
            (2). Walter the Penniless
         b. Outcome
      2. The Princes' Crusade
         a. Leaders
            (1). Godfrey of Buillon
            (2). Raymond of Toulouse
            (3). Bohemund
            (4). Robert of Normandy
         b. Accomplishments
            (1). Capture of Nicaea
            (2). Capture of Antioch
            (3). Capture of Jerusalem
               (a). Destruction of buildings
               (b). Massacre of Saracens
            (4). Organization of Jerusalem
               (a). Godfrey
               (b). Baldwin I
               (c). Baldwin II
               (d). Baldwin III

     B. The Second Crusade
        1. Influences
        2. Leaders
           a. Conrad
           b. Louis
        3. Outcome
           a. Siege of Damascus
           b. Failure of siege
           c. Discredit of movement
           d. Fall of Jerusalem

[The remaining topics under II are omitted here. In the complete outline the subordinate topics of II, C through I ("The Eighth Crusade"), were given with further subordination, following the general pattern established in II A and B.]

III. The results
     A. Unity of classes of society
     B. Downfall of feudalism
     C. Rise of new orders
     D. Increase in wealth of church
     E. Creation of new literature
     F. Introduction of Eastern culture

Fig. 12, An Example of Evaluation [Griffith Thompson Pugh, "The Crusades," *Guide to Research Writing*, pp. 43–44, Houghton Mifflin Company. New York: 1955. Used by permission].

"The principle of organization for the main topic of 'The Crusades' is that of *cause and effect*. The first topic is entirely cause; the second topic is the effect of the first and the cause of the third; the third topic is entirely effect. *Chronology* [time] determines the order of subordinate topics of the first importance under the second main topic. These subordinate topics are developed internally by *another logical arrangement* that has the same general pattern, usually, for each part, but varies to accommodate the differences in materials. Even *spatial* [space] arrangement is used in the outline—for example, in the topics under II A 2 b, which are concerned with the accomplishments of the Princes' Crusade. The outline illustrates good organization.

"The outline also illustrates correct form. Main topics begin at the margin and each degree of subordination is indicated by the proper indention. Topics are placed in logical order, and are numbered or lettered according to their order and importance. There are no predications, as in a sentence outline; each topic is worded as a substantive. Parallelism is properly observed in the wording of the topics within each group: main topics, subordinate topics under each main topic, and so on. Every subordinate topic is parallel to others in its immediate group. Punctuation is consistent: a period is placed after the symbol before each topic; end punctuation following the topics is omitted.

"A weakness in the outline is the lack of clarity in the thought relationships between topic II A 2 b (4) and the topics subordinate to it. The reader may wonder how Godfrey or Baldwin I is subordinate to 'Organization of Jerusalem.' For the most part, however, the outline, which was prepared by a student, is clear, and the thought relationships are easily discernible." [1]

A *check list for evaluation*

To be an effective tool for writing, an outline must meet these requirements: (1) the major divisions of the outline must equal the content of the entire subject; (2) the subdivisions of any part of the outline must equal that part of the subject; (3) no division of the outline should overlap any other division of the outline.

Figure 13, following, is a check list that will aid you in checking your outline to see whether your plan for writing is logical and coherent.

A CHECK LIST FOR EVALUATING AN OUTLINE

1. Have all vague, general headings such as "Introduction" and "Conclusion" been replaced with specific, completely developed headings?
2. Has the outline been properly consolidated by reducing major divisions to a minimum?
3. Do the major topic headings clearly show the essential division of the subject, their order, and their relationships?
4. Are all of the subordinate headings logically dependent on the headings immediately superior to them?
5. Are all coordinate headings of equal weight (and importance)?
6. Are all coordinate headings within a given section worded in parallel fashion?
7. Have all single headings (or divisions) under larger headings been eliminated or incorporated into the larger heading?
8. Is the amount of space devoted to the various sections of the outline proportionate to their relative importance to the subject and the relative amount of space they will be given in the finished paper?

Fig. 13, A Check List for Evaluating an Outline.

[1] Griffith Thompson Pugh, *Guide to Research Writing*, p. 44, Houghton Mifflin Company. New York: 1955. Used by permission.

4

Principles and Patterns of Organization

Organization is the most difficult and important aspect of writing. It is the basis of clarity. Without organization, the ideas and information in a paper are unrelated and therefore confusing.

Organization consists of two steps, division and arrangement. Most writers fail to realize this and so have difficulty outlining.

To organize your outline, first divide your subject into categories; then arrange these categories in their natural or logical order. Next, subdivide each category and arrange its topics (or headings) in their natural or logical order. Each category can have a different arrangement from every other category. Therefore, synthesizing your outline to give it a feeling of unity is often quite difficult.

In part, this difficulty stems from the fact that the processes of division and arrangement are so similar and so often performed simultaneously that most writers tend to think of them as one. For simple subjects that have an obvious natural division, the problem is not acute: you can perform both processes at the same time without difficulty. But for complex subjects, the two processes must (for the most part) be performed separately, for if you think of them as one, you will have difficulty organizing your outline.

In organizing (as in war), you must divide to conquer. The division of your subject into its major topics will help you to see its structure (the relationship of its parts). This division of your subject should be based on classification or analysis, whichever applies.

Once you have divided the subject, arrange its topics in the order that will best enable your reader to understand, remember, and use the information presented. Since some patterns of arrangement are similar to or overlap others, you may find it difficult, at times, to make the proper choice.

Division

Division is of two types, analysis and classification. Analysis is the division of formless subjects into their possible (or plausible) parts. Classification, on the other hand, is the division of subjects that have a definite form into their major categories according to the basis of relationship common to all of the categories.

Analysis

Analysis is the division of formless subjects into their possible (or plausible) parts through the use of experimentation, experience, and imagination.

Experimentation (or trial and error) is often the quickest means of determining the major divisions of simple subjects. Set down what you know about the subject, as you would for a scratch outline; then try to pick out the major divisions from the points listed, taking into consideration all of the possibilities that experience, knowledge, and imagination suggest.

Famous Americans is such a formless subject that requires analysis to divide it into its component parts. To analyze this subject, you must first define (or decide) what you mean by *famous*. You may even have to define *Americans*; do you mean both North and South Americans or just citizens of the United States? If you mean only the latter, should you include Colonists who died before 1776 or only those who were alive after that date? If you limit the subject to citizens of the United States from Colonial times to the present, you can divide it in a number of ways: according to fields of achievement (literature, politics, business); chronological periods (Colonial days, the Civil War); geographical areas (the North, the Midwest); importance (presidents, inventors, business executives); and so forth. Which of these methods of division you choose will depend on your purpose for writing, your knowledge of the subject, the reader's need for the information, and the degree to which the subject is to be developed.

You may decide to divide the subject into its major topics from several points of view. You may first divide the subject of *Famous Americans* alphabetically according to fields of achievement (art, business, government) and then list the individuals in each of these categories chronologically, according to their dates of birth.

Classification

Classification is the division of a subject into categories, each of which has a common relationship (or common denominator). In classification, first divide the subject into categories according to their form, function, use, characteristics, condition, or other basis of relationship. Then divide these major categories (or topics) into subtopics, according to the degree of development necessary to explain the subject clearly to the reader. This division of the subject into topics (major headings) and subtopics (subordinate headings) enables you to discuss the subject in small, easily-manageable bites.

The value of classification is that related ideas are more quickly understood by the reader than are unrelated ideas. Classification permits you to arrange related facts, ideas, or objects in groups to give them a sense of order and to point up their similarities. It also aids you in the formulation of general conclusions, principles, and premises.

Classification is dependent on your knowledge of a subject and the ways in which it can be viewed (or divided). The subject *dogs*, for instance, can be divided in a number of ways: according to types (collies, terriers, poodles), according to function (hunting dogs, work dogs, show dogs, pets), according to country of origin, and the like.

From one point of view, *language* can be divided into the following categories: words, phrases, clauses, sentences, paragraphs, and so forth. Each of these subdivisions, in turn, can be divided either as a part of the overall subject or as a separate subject itself. Figure 14, following, illustrates how the subject *language* could be divided from this viewpoint.

LANGUAGE

I. Words
  A. Nouns
    1. Classes
      a. Common
        1. Concrete
          a. Tree
          b. Trunk
          c. Limb
          d. Branch
          e. Twig
          f. Leaf
        2. Mass
        3. Abstract
        4. Collective
      b. Proper
    2. Position & Function
    3. Forms
  B. Pronouns
  C. Verbs
  D. Adjectives
  E. Adverbs
  F. Prepositions
  G. Conjunctions
  H. Interjections
II. Phrases
III. Clauses
IV. Sentences
V. Paragraphs
VI. Paper

This is, of course, a fragmentary breakdown. A complete breakdown of such a complex subject would take many pages. Only *words* is subdivided to any degree. It is arranged according to the order of enumeration, which is used also for the arrangement of *classes* and *common*. *Concrete* is arranged according to the order of decreasing importance. The overall subject is arranged according to the order of increasing importance.

Fig. 14, An Example of Classification.

Arrangement

All writing should be arranged according to some basis of natural or logical order. Natural order is the order inherent in the subject. Logical order, on the other hand, is the order imposed on the subject by the writer and is based on inference (or reason).

An outline is a type of summary that lists the components of a subject according to their natural or logical order. In making an outline, you should use the order of arrangement that is best suited to the information being presented and the type of writing being done. Remember that each category can have a different order of arrangement from every other category in the outline.

The most common types of arrangement are time order, space order, order of importance, cause-effect order, general-particular order, and enumeration. The other types of arrangement are largely variations or combinations of these; therefore, distinct lines of demarcation are difficult to draw between them.

Time order

When using time (or chronological) order, begin your paper at a specific date or period of time and move forward or backward from minute-to-minute, hour-to-hour, day-to-day, year-to-year, or other unit of time. In an historical report, for example, you can start at the beginning of an era or event and proceed in time to its conclusion, or you may start at its climax and work backward in time to its beginning.

Your point of view with respect to the subject will determine, in part, your choice of order. In writing about the events of a given day, for example, you can logically begin your discussion of that day either at midnight, at dawn, or at eight o'clock in the morning. Or you can take up your discussion as of three o'clock in the afternoon if that is the time at which the events of the day had their real beginning. Your discussion can proceed either from minute-to-minute or hour-to-hour or in larger, less definite units such as morning, afternoon, evening, night.

Time order is, obviously, most effective in papers in which the emphasis is on the time relationship. It is the arrangement traditionally used in narration, historical papers and reports, biography and autobiography.

Figure 15, following, illustrates how Texas history can be divided into nine major time periods on the basis of the six flags that have flown over the state. [No numbering system is used to avoid confusion with the dates, which serve as a satisfactory numbering system themselves, and only the first Spanish period is to any degree developed.]

SIX FLAGS OVER TEXAS

1519–1685   Spain
    1519   DePineda's exploration of the Texas coast
    1528   De Vaca shipwrecked on the Texas coast
    1541   Coronado's march across Texas
    1542   De Soto's men reach Texas
    1680   Missions and settlements established near El Paso
1685–1690   France
1690–1821   Spain
1821–1836   Mexico
1836–1845   The Republic of Texas
1845–1861   The United States
1861–1865   The Confederacy
1865–1874   The Reconstruction Era (The United States)
1870–   The United States

Fig. 15, An Example of Time Order.

Even though the major divisions of your paper are arranged chronologically, you can develop other sections according to different types of order, for example, according to the importance of the event to the rise or fall of the country involved.

Time order is often combined with space order as in operational order. Except for minor sections, time order is usually ineffective for the arrangement of complex subjects.

Figure 16 is an example of time order presented in vertical tabular form. Vertical tabular form and horizontal tabular form [see Fig. 18, p. 44] will aid you in visualizing relationships within a subject that occur (or occurred) at the same time (or at overlapping times) in the same place (or at different places). As part of the information has to be "tacked onto" other headings or listed under the headings, crowding the items and causing confusion, such outlines are hard to develop in detail. Therefore, once you "see" the relationships through the use of vertical or horizontal form, you will usually find it helpful to "translate" these outlines into conventional outline form before you begin to write.

Vertical tabular form is commonly used for tables of organization, genealogical tables [see Fig. 16], and the like.

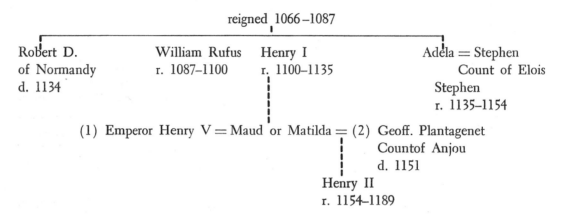

Fig. 16, An Example of Vertical Tabular Form.

Space order

Space (or geographical) order is used for papers than can be explained according to spatial relationships: from north to south, east to west, front to back, top to bottom, side to side, interior to exterior, floor to floor, and so forth. Begin your paper by describing an object, usually starting from a fixed point as the reader sees it.

Space order can be used to explain the relationships between the various offices or departments within a business or industry, the arrangement of a building, the divisions of an assembly line, and the like. It can also be used for travel articles, guide books, and geographies.

Figure 17, following, is an example of space order.

A TRIP ALONG THE PACIFIC COAST

I. The Pacific Coast
  A. Washington
  B. Oregon
  C. California
II. Washington
  A. Seattle
  B. Tacoma
  C. Olympia
III. Oregon
  A. Portland
  B. Klamath Falls
IV. California
  A. San Francisco
    1. Twin Peaks
    2. Seal Rocks
    3. Golden Gate Park
      a. Windmills
      b. Lakes
      c. Rainbow Falls
      d. Redwood Grove
    4. Chinatown
    5. Fisherman's Wharf
    6. Nob Hill
  B. Los Angeles
  C. San Diego

Only the section under San Francisco is developed in detail. Points of interest between the cities could also be listed. Under San Francisco, the view of the surrounding city, the bay, and the ocean could be described so that the reader could see the spatial relationships between the various sights when each is mentioned later. Golden Gate Park has some fifty points of interest, all of which could be brought out or, as is done here, representative examples could be selected, either to emphasize the ones selected or to suggest the whole, since space limitations do not permit the inclusion of all fifty.

Fig. 17, An Example of Space Order.

Figure 18 is an example of space order presented in horizontal tabular form. Like vertical tabular form, horizontal tabular form will aid you in visualizing operations that are carried out simultaneously or things occurring at the same time or at overlapping times in different places. A time relationship is inherent in Figure 18, and approximate dates could be included under or following each item.

PROTO-GERMANIC FAMILY OF LANGUAGES

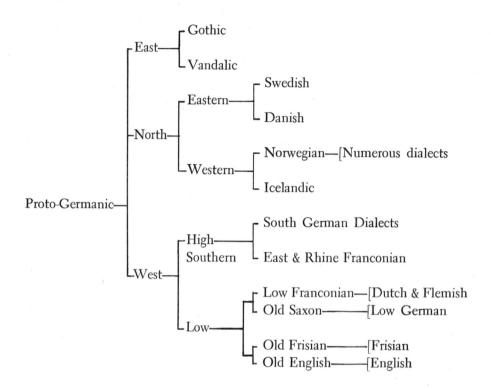

Fig. 18, An Example of Horizontal Tabular Form.

Operational order

Operational order (or the order of manufacturing sequence) is essentially a combination of time and space order. It is commonly used for subjects that have a sequence of operation such as the explanation of a process [see Fig. 39, p. 69], the operation of a piece of equipment, and how-to-do-it articles. It is used (as in a flow chart) to trace the step-by-step development of a product (or a raw material) through a plant, telling the steps performed, the order of their performance, the time required for each step, and the place in the plant or the assembly line where the step is performed.

In operational order, emphasis can be placed on either time or space order, or both may be emphasized equally. On occasion, time order is violated in this type of arrangement, as two operations that are performed simultaneously must, of necessity, be discussed separately.

In operational order, you normally take up the various parts of a machine or the steps in a process in their order of performance. The description of the operation can be either internal or external, depending on whether you begin with the inner or the outer workings of the machine or process if there is a choice. The paper concerns *what* happens, *where* it happens, *when* it happens, and *how* it is done. At times, *why* something is done is also reported, as in functional order.

Figure 19, following, is an example of operational order in which the emphasis is primarily on the time relationship. The outline could be developed in detail in paragraph form or presented in its existing form in a book on handicraft if conventional techniques such as burnishing are explained elsewhere in the text.

HOW TO MAKE A CHAIN LINK BRACELET

1. The tools used to make a chain link bracelet, in the order of use, are as follows:

    1.1   A bench vise.
    1.2   A ½″ wood dowel, 10″ long.
    1.3   A jeweler's saw.
    1.4   A pair of 4½″ flat-nosed pliers.
    1.5   A pickle bath.
    1.6   Solder flux.
    1.7   Silver solder.
    1.8   A charcoal block.
    1.9   A jeweler's blow torch.
    1.10 A needle file.
    1.11 A burnisher.

    Headings in a sentence outline do not have to be complete sentences so long as they form complete sentences with the preceding larger heading. Note that a period follows each topic heading.

2. The materials required, in the order of use, are the following:
    2.1   #7 silver wire.
    2.2   A ready-made clasp.
    2.3   Binding wire.
3. The steps to be performed, in order, are as follows:
    3.1   Fasten the dowel and one end of the wire in the bench vise.
    3.2   Coil the silver wire tightly around the dowel.
    3.3   Make 12 to 16 complete turns, depending on the required size of the bracelet when completed.
    3.4   Remove the dowel from the vise and slip the coil from the dowel [permissible compound heading].
    3.5   Fasten the coil lightly in the vise and saw through the coil lengthwise, forming 12 to 16 links, depending on the number of turns taken.
    3.6   Remove the links from the vise and open them with the pliers so that they can be joined [permissible compound heading].

3.7   Join the links, forming a chain; then close them using the pliers [permissible compound heading].

3.8   Clean the endlinks in the pickle bath using standard procedure.

3.9   Brush the solder flux on these links at the points where the clasp is to be attached; then wire the two sections of the clasp to the links using the binding wire [permissible compound heading].

3.10 Solder the clasp to the links using standard procedure.

3.11 Solder links also, if desired, for greater security.

3.12 Clean the bracelet in the pickel bath.

3.13 Remove excess solder with the file.

3.14 Clean, burnish, and polish the bracelet using standard procedures.

Fig. 19, An Example of Operational Order.

Functional order

Because *function* and *functional* are at times used as synonyms for *operation* and *operational* and because operational order and functional order are often used in combination, it is necessary to make a distinction between the two to avoid confusion. In operational order, you tell what *is* done and *how* it is done. In functional order, you tell what *is supposed to be* done and *why*. In essence, *function* is synonymous with *purpose* (or *reason*).

Operational and functional order are often combined to tell what is done and how and why. To put it simply, the function of your hand is to grasp, and the operation of your hand is how it grasps (or the way in which it grasps: the interplay of muscles, tendons, and bones and the opposition of the thumb and fingers).

Functional order is commonly used for the major divisions of an outline, and each major division is then developed in operational order. In the example of functional order given in Figure 20, following, only section II is developed in detail.

THE USES OF OUTLINING

I. Outlining is a method of determining (or clarifying) your paper's purpose.

II. Outlining is a means of testing your paper's organization.

    A. A poorly organized paper will not be completely successful no matter how well it is written.

    B. The outline provides an effective test of your paper's organization before it is ever written, since it is the skeleton of the paper.

        1. The outline should be checked carefully for weaknesses in its structure.

            a. All major divisions should be checked against the thesis to determine their relevancy.

            b. All like divisions should be checked against one another to see if they overlap, if there are any gaps in reasoning, and if they are in proper order.

        2. All weaknesses in the outline should be corrected before you begin to write.

III. Outlining is a means of complete communication [for example, Fig. 19, p. 45, can stand alone in a handicraft text].

IV. Outlining is an aid in writing.

V. Outlining is an aid to reading, through abstracting someone else's paper or report [see Fig. 36, p. 65].

Fig. 20, An Example of Functional Order.

It should be emphasized that there is no one approach to presenting, organizing, or developing a subject. The units of the army as a whole—the infantry soldier, the rifle platoon, the headquarters company, the tank battalion, for example—can be discussed according to functional order (what they are supposed to do), operational order (how they are supposed to do it), or organizational order (the makeup of the units to enable them to perform their respective duties or functions).

Organizational order

In organizational order, you discuss the various divisions of an organization that enable it to perform its basic function (or purpose). You can arrange the divisions of the organization according to whatever basis seems the most natural or logical. At times, your choice of arrangement will be arbitrary as in enumeration. At other times, it will be according to their order of importance.

For example, in discussing the officers of an organization (listing their duties, responsibilities, and so forth), you would discuss the various officers in the order of their decreasing importance—president, vice president, secretary, treasurer, parliamentarian, sergeant-at-arms. This is also the order in which they are traditionally presented [see Traditional order, p. 71].

Figure 21, following, is an example of such traditional organizational order.

THE BRANCHES OF THE FEDERAL GOVERNMENT

I. The Executive
   A. The President
   B. The Vice President
   C. The Cabinet
      1. The Secretary of State
      2. The Secretary of the Treasury
II. The Legislative (Congress)
   A. The Senate
   B. The House of Representatives
III. The Judiciary
   A. The Supreme Court
   B. The Lower Federal Courts

This is a fragmentary breakdown. The cabinet is not given in its entirety, and executive agencies and the breakdown of the federal courts are omitted.

Fig. 21, An Example of Organizational Order.

The breakdown of the army (given in the order of increasing importance in Figure 22, page 49) is an example of organizational order also. Thus the overlapping of different types of order that often occurs can be clearly seen.

Order of increasing importance

In the order of increasing (or ascending) importance, present the points, ideas, facts, or opinions that make up your subject in the order of their increasing importance, size, denomination, weight, value, degree, emotional impact, or the like. For this reason, it is also referred to as the order of climax. For example, if a production engineer wishes to explain why he chose one process of manufacturing a product in preference to the other choices available to him, he might start by eliminating the least effective process, then the next to the least effective, and so on until he reached the most effective process.

Figure 22, following, is an example of the order of increasing importance.

THE ARMY

I. Soldier
    A. Enlisted men
        1. Recruit
        2. Private
        3. Private First Class
        4. Specialist 4
        5. Corporal
        6. Specialist 5
        7. Sergeant
        8. Specialist 6
        9. Staff Sergeant
        10. Specialist 7
        11. Platoon Sergeant
        12. Sergeant First Class
        13. Specialist 8
        14. First Sergeant
        15. Master Sergeant
        16. Specialist 9
        17. Sergeant Major
    B. Warrant Officers
        1. Warrant Officer, W-1
        2. Chief Warrant Officer, W-2
        3. Chief Warrant Officer, W-3
        4. Chief Warrant Officer, W-4
    C. Officers
        1. 2nd Lieutenant
        2. 1st Lieutenant
        3. Captain
        4. Major
        5. Lieutenant Colonel
        6. Colonel
        7. Brigadier General
        8. Major General
        9. Lieutenant General
        10. General
        11. General of the Army
II. Squad
III. Platoon
IV. Company
V. Battalion
VI. Regiment
VII. Brigade
VIII. Division
IX. Corps
X. Army

Only *soldier* is developed in any detail. Each rank and grade could be developed according to duties, privileges, and pay and according to the requirements for the rank or grade.

This is also an example of organizational order.

Fig. 22, An Example of the Order of Increasing Importance.

Order of decreasing importance

In the order of decreasing (or descending) importance, present the points, ideas, facts, or opinions that make up your subject in the order of their decreasing importance, size, denomination, weight, value, degree, emotional impact, or the like. Although this often gives your writing a feeling of anticlimax, some types of scientific and engineering articles, papers, and reports require its use. Newspaper stories are traditionally written in this way so that if a story has to be cut, the editor can lop off the unimportant information at the end of the story without having to stop to make a value judgment of the information included; for these examples, therefore, it is also traditional order.

If a production engineer wishes to begin his report with what he considers to be the best method of manufacture and then tell why he eliminated other methods available to him, he could present the various methods of manufacture in their decreasing order of importance.

Figure 23, following, is an example of the order of decreasing importance combined with the order of effect to cause.

CAUSES OF AUTO ACCIDENTS

I. Causes of auto accidents according to decreasing frequency
   A. Human failure
   B. Mechanical failure
   C. Other causes
II. Human failure according to decreasing frequency
   A. Traveling too fast
   B. Following too close
   C. Intoxication (may be a contributing factor to other causes)
   D. Failure to yield right-of-way
   E. Driving on the wrong side of the road
   F. Running stoplights
   G. Falling asleep at the wheel
   H. Pulling onto the highway from the shoulder too quickly
III. Mechanical failure according to decreasing frequency
   A. Blowouts
   B. Brake failure
      1. Foot brake
         a. Brakes wet
         b. Brake lining wornout
         c. Loss of brake fluid

        2. Hand brake
            a. Brake faulty
            b. Brake not set
            c. Brake improperly set
IV. Other causes according to decreasing frequency
    A. Slick or icy pavement
    B. Children running in front of cars
    C. Unmarked road hazards
    D. Driver blinded by oncoming lights

Fig. 23, An Example of the Order of Decreasing Importance.

Order of cause to effect

The order of cause to effect is used to explain why something happened or to predict what will happen. In the order of cause to effect, discuss the facts, forces, statistics, and ideas that make up your subject; then show their effect and explain why they caused this effect. Or list the information; then predict what will happen as a result. In this respect, the cause-effect relationship is similar to the order of particular to general. Cause-effect order is commonly used to explain phenomena in such fields as chemistry, physics, sociology, and history [see Fig. 12, p. 34].

There is a tendency when using cause-effect order to oversimplify; therefore, several factors should be kept in mind when using this arrangement:

1. An effect can have several causes.

2. An effect can become a cause.

3. A cause may have more than one effect.

For instance, a man's drunkenness may stem from his basic feeling of insecurity, his competition with younger men, and money problems. In turn, his drunkenness may lead to his loss of self-respect, the loss of his job, and separation from his family.

This continuing cause-effect relationship can set up a chain reaction as follows: two men have a difference of opinion; this leads to an argument, which results in name calling, which causes a fight, which results in one of the men having a heart attack, which causes the man's death, which leads to the other man's arrest and a court action being taken against him, which results in a jail sentence for manslaughter. Even this jail sentence is not necessarily the end. It will cause still other effects: on his family, his attitude toward society, his ability to get a job on his release from jail; these (in turn) will result in etcetera, etcetera, etcetera.

Figure 24, following, illustrates a series of joint causes that result in one effect, a strike, which (in turn) is the cause of a series of effects.

Cause-effect order can be combined with other types of order. For example, it can be combined with time order by relating the causes in the order of their occurrence, or it can be related to space order by relating where the causes and their effects took place.

STRIKES: THEIR CAUSES AND EFFECTS

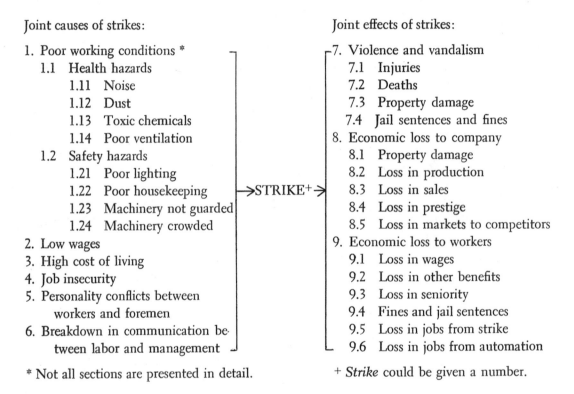

Joint causes of strikes:

1. Poor working conditions *
   1.1   Health hazards
      1.11   Noise
      1.12   Dust
      1.13   Toxic chemicals
      1.14   Poor ventilation
   1.2   Safety hazards
      1.21   Poor lighting
      1.22   Poor housekeeping
      1.23   Machinery not guarded
      1.24   Machinery crowded
2. Low wages
3. High cost of living
4. Job insecurity
5. Personality conflicts between workers and foremen
6. Breakdown in communication between labor and management

→STRIKE+→

Joint effects of strikes:

7. Violence and vandalism
   7.1   Injuries
   7.2   Deaths
   7.3   Property damage
   7.4   Jail sentences and fines
8. Economic loss to company
   8.1   Property damage
   8.2   Loss in production
   8.3   Loss in sales
   8.4   Loss in prestige
   8.5   Loss in markets to competitors
9. Economic loss to workers
   9.1   Loss in wages
   9.2   Loss in other benefits
   9.3   Loss in seniority
   9.4   Fines and jail sentences
   9.5   Loss in jobs from strike
   9.6   Loss in jobs from automation

* Not all sections are presented in detail.   + *Strike* could be given a number.

Fig. 24, An Example of the Order of Cause to Effect.

Order of effect to cause

In the order of effect to cause, start with the presentation of a problem, an effect, or a condition; then discuss its probable cause or causes. In this respect, the effect to cause arrangement is similar to both problem-solution order and the order of general to particular.

Figure 25, following, is an example of the order of effect to cause in which only section II is presented in detail.

DISEASES OF THE HEART

I. Types of diseases of the heart
II. Diseases of the valves of the heart
   A. Inflamation of the valves
      1. Effects of inflamation
         a. Damage to one or more valves causing them to leak
         b. Formation of scar tissue resulting in narrowing of the valves, causing incompetence or stenosis or both
      2. Causes of inflamation
         a. Rheumatism in children and young adults
         b. Valves attacked by pneumococci, pyogenic streptococci and staphylococci, gonococci, and influenza bacilli
   B. Lesions of the valves—heart murmurs
      1. Types of lesions, or heart murmurs
         a. Mitral valve—murmur at the apex beat
         b. Aortic valve—murmur in the second right intercostal space
      2. Effects of lesions, or heart murmurs
         a. Hypertrophy
         b. Compensation
         c. Breakdown of compensation resulting in dropsy, cyanosis, coughing, or shortness of breath
      3. Causes of lesions, or heart murmurs
         a. Stenosis
         b. Incompetence
III. Disease of the walls of the heart
IV. Disorders of rhythm of the heart's action

Fig. 25, An Example of the Order of Effect to Cause.

Order of particular to general

In the order of particular to general (as in inductive reasoning), develop your subject by presenting a series of facts, points, ideas, or cases from which you draw a conclusion, law, proposition, or premise. Take up these facts (points, ideas, or cases) in the order of their use (or occurrence); then build to a conclusion in which you draw them together.

When describing an experiment, for example, a chemist may present the steps that led him to a general conclusion (or result). In social welfare work, an investigator may present a series of evaluations about a particular case (the individual's personality, skills, difficulties, family, associates, and environment) and lead up to a general conclusion about the individual.

In this type of order, the reader is given a list of clues (facts, evidence, instances, or examples) that will enable him to discover the conclusion for himself. He is led to this conclusion by the step-by-step presentation of the clues given. For this reason, it is an excellent pattern for narration and much used in detective and mystery stories.

A doctor often follows this pattern of reasoning when examining a patient.

Symptoms (particular facts, or clues)

Double vision

Drooping of eyelids

Difficulty in swallowing

Difficulty in respiration

Extreme muscular weakness

Diagnosis (general conclusion)

Botulism

Having diagnosed botulism in a group of people, the doctor could follow the same pattern of reasoning to determine its cause.

Food eaten by each patient (particular facts)

#1: sausage, potato salad, green beans

#2: ham, potato chips, green beans

#3: beef, french fries, green beans

Cause of botulism (general conclusion)

Green beans

The order of particular to general offers a more specific development than does its opposite number. Since it starts with details rather than ideas and builds to a climax, it is more exciting and suspenseful than the order of general to particular. But since the reader does not know from the outset the direction in which these details are supposed to lead him, he may become lost. Therefore, it is not normally recommended for technical or scientific writing. This difficulty can be overcome in part, however, if you begin with the conclusion, even though the conclusion can logically be drawn only from a careful study of the facts that follow.

The order of particular to general is difficult to set down in outline form, which commonly begins each major section with a general statement and proceeds to an increasingly detailed development of this statement. One means of overcoming this difficulty is to start each major section with a question, followed by details which support or disprove the question. The section is then concluded with a statement that summarizes these details.

Figure 26, following, is an example of this pattern of arrangement. Both the outline as a whole and the individual major sections are developed in particular to general order. The symbol ∴ [*therefore*] is used, rather than a capital letter, to set off the conclusions more clearly.

DO JEWS CONTROL THE AMERICAN ECONOMY?

I. Do Jews control the American economy or is their alleged control a myth?
II. Do Jews control banking and finance?
    A. Jews are not an important factor in commercial or investment banking.
    B. Nor are they an important factor in such related fields as insurance.
    ∴ Jews do not control banking and finance.
III. Do Jews control heavy industry?
    A. Jews are an important factor in the scrap-iron business and the waste-products industry, which are on the borderline of heavy industry.
    B. They are not an important factor in such fields as chemicals, petroleum, building, and transportation.
    C. Neither are they an important factor in the field of private utilities.
    D. Nor are they an important factor in the area of natural resources.
    ∴ They do not control heavy industry.
IV. Do Jews control light industry?
    A. Jewish control of light industry is largely limited to the area of distribution.
    B. Their influence in the area of manufacture is slight.
    ∴ Jews do not dominate light industry.
V. Do Jews control the field of communications?
    A. Jews control few major magazines.
    B. They are an important factor in book publishing and printing.
    C. They have a significant measure of control in radio, television, motion pictures, and the field of entertainment.
    ∴ Jews are an important factor in the field of communications.
VI. ∴ Although Jews dominate some areas of the economy, their alleged control of the American economy is a myth.

Fig. 26, An Example of the Order of Particular to General [Carey McWilliams, "The Marginal Man," *A Mask of Privilege: Anti-Semitism in America*, pp. 42–48, Little, Brown and Co. Boston: 1947. Used by permission].

In the original, the statements made in Figure 26 are supported by evidence and developed in detail which cannot be included here.

Order of general to particular

The order of general to particular is the basic order of exposition and outline form. In this order (as in deductive reasoning), develop your subject by starting with a conclusion, law, proposition, or premise which you then develop (or support) with individual points of evidence (or examples).

The order of general to particular offers a greater degree of clarity than does its opposite number, since the reader is told at the outset what the paper (or the individual section or paragraph) is about, then given evidence, examples, illustrations, and a step-by-step explanation to support this introductory statement.

The order of general to particular is similar to the order of effect to cause and can be used in combination with other types of order such as the order of decreasing importance. In the case in which the doctor diagnosed botulism (the effect) and determined green beans to be its cause, the order of effect to cause and the order of general to particular are essentially the same. General to particular order can also be combined with time order, space order, the order of increasing importance, and the like. For instance, this paragraph is an example of the order of general to particular as used in exposition.

Figure 27, following, is an example of general to particular order. It is also a reversal of Figure 26, page 55, showing how the same information can be presented from two points of view.

JEWS AND THE AMERICAN ECONOMY

I. The alleged control of the American economy by the Jews is a myth.
II. Jews do not control banking and finance.
    A. Jews are not an important factor in either commercial or investment banking.
    B. Nor are they an important factor in such related fields as insurance.
III. Jews do not control heavy industry.
    A. Jews are an important factor in the scrap-iron business and the waste-products industry, which are on the border-line of heavy industry.
    B. They are not an important factor in such fields as chemicals, petroleum, building, and transportation.
    C. Neither are they an important factor in the field of private utilities.
    D. Nor are they an important factor in the area of natural resources.
IV. Jews do not dominate light industry.
    A. Jewish control of light industry is largely limited to the area of distribution.
    B. Their influence in the area of manufacturing is slight.

V. Jews largely dominate the field of communications.
   A. Jews control few major magazines.
   B. They are an important factor in book publishing and printing.
   C. They have a significant measure of control in radio, television, motion pictures, and the field of entertainment.
VI. Although Jews dominate some areas of the nation's economy, their alleged control of the American economy is a myth.

Fig. 27, An Example of the Order of General to Particular [McWilliams, A *Mask of Privilege*, pp. 42–48].

Figure 27 is also an informative abstract of the original in outline form.

Enumeration

Enumeration (like analysis) is the arrangement of formless subjects (or of formless sections of a subject) in some convenient sequence. In most instances, this arrangement is based largely on your arbitrary choice of what to set down first, second, third, and so on as in a list. For this reason, it is sometimes referred to as the order of choice. At times, however, you can use some simple device such as alphabetical order for the arrangement of the various items, as in a bibliography, which is arranged alphabetically according to the authors' surnames or the first important word in the titles. Such devices should be used sparingly, however, as they provide little subtlety of presentation.

Though all of the parts of a subject do not have a direct basis of relationship, two or more may, and these should be arranged according to their natural or logical order. At times, the order used for these related parts can be used to tie all of the parts rather loosely together. For instance, if several of the points lend themselves to arrangement according to qualities (hot or cold) or values (best or worst), the order of increasing or decreasing importance could be used to establish a basic arrangement, but such arrangements should not be used if they are obviously forced.

At times, imagination can provide a basis for arrangement. For example, a discussion of different types of dogs could be arranged alphabetically (Afghans, bassets, beagles, collies), but a more imaginative and interesting arrangement could be made on the basis of increasing or decreasing importance according to the popularity of the various breeds or chronologically according to the ages of the breeds or their average life spans.

The parts of speech in a discussion of language could be arranged alphabetically, but a better arrangement would be noun, pronoun, verb, adjective, adverb, proposition, conjunction, and interjection, which relates noun and pronoun, adjective and adverb, and preposition and conjunctions, which have certain functional similarities.

Figure 28, following, is an example of the use of the ABC's as a basis for organization. It is also an example of symbolical unity.

THE ABC'S OF GETTING ALONG WITH TEENAGE DAUGHTERS

I. Because business has gone all out to flatter teenagers' egos "en route to their pocketbooks," many teenagers think they deserve all kinds of privileges without having to work for them.
  A. The teens are the age when girls turn away from their mothers and learn to stand on their own feet.
  B. The teens are also the age when girls need guidance more than at any other time.
II. Here are some ABC's for coping with a teenage daughter.
  A. Appeal to her idealism.
  B. Bear in mind that you're still the boss.
  C. Consideration is a two-way street.
     [All other headings except the last are omitted here.]
XYZ. XYZ stand for the unknowns that face your daughter in the life ahead.

Fig. 28, An Example of Enumeration—1 [Dr. Joyce Brothers, "The ABC's of Getting Along with Teenage Daughters," *Good Housekeeping*, October 1965, vol. 161, no. 1, pp. 56, 58–59. Used by permission].

The annual report of a company, Figure 29, following, is a typical formless subject that must be arranged according to some basis of enumeration, usually according to some traditional order.

ANNUAL REPORT OF A UTILITY COMPANY

1. To the stockholders
2. Personnel
  2.1 Executives
  2.2 Employees
3. Expansion
  3.1 Territory
  3.2 Sales
4. Summary of operations
  4.1 Operating expenses
  4.2 Operating revenues
5. Balance sheet

Fig. 29, An Example of Enumeration—2.

Such an annual report could be made more interesting with an imaginative presentation. All of the preliminary information of the report is a build up to the balance sheet, since the basic reason for such a report is to show the company's financial position. To underline its purpose, therefore, the report could be presented under the overall headings "Debits" and "Credits."

A paper whose major sections are arranged on the basis of enumeration can have any or all of its major sections developed on the basis of some other type or types of order.

A paper whose major sections are arranged according to some basis other than enumeration can have one or more of its sections developed according to enumeration.

Problem-solution order

In problem-solution order, first describe (or discuss) a problem; then present its solution or possible solution. If you wish, you can divide the discussion into just two major headings: the problem and the solution.

The steps in problem solving are (1) recognition of the problem; (2) analysis of the problem; (3) definition of the problem; (4) determination of its possible solution or solutions (based on observation, study, and research); (5) testing the possible solution (or solutions); (6) drawing conclusions; (7) making recommendations.

When there is more than one possible solution to the problem, problem-solution is similar to comparison and contrast and to pro and con arrangement.

Figure 30, following, illustrates two patterns of arrangement that can be used for problem-solution order.

PATTERNS OF PROBLEM-SOLUTION

Problem-solution Pattern—1
Problem
  Effect
  Probable cause(s)
  Tests to determine cause(s)
    Methods (procedures)
    Means (materials, etc.)
Solution
  Methods (procedures)
  Means (materials, etc.)
Conclusions and recommendations

Problem-solution Pattern—2
Problem
  Effect
  Cause(s)
Solution 1
  Methods (procedures)
  Means (materials, etc.)
Solution 2
  Methods (procedures)
  Means (materials, etc.)
Recommended solution

Fig. 30, Examples of Patterns of Problem-solution.

Problem-solution follows the order of effect to cause in the development of the problem, but it can go beyond the simple effect to cause relationship, as is shown in Figure 31, following, which is an extension of Figure 24, page 52.

STRIKE: CAUSE, EFFECT, SOLUTION

1. Problem: labor-management differences
    1.1   Effect: strike
    1.2   Causes
        1.21   Poor working conditions
        1.22   Low wages
        1.23   High cost of living
        1.24   Job insecurity
        1.25   Personality conflicts between workers and foreman
        1.26   Breakdown of communication between labor and management
2. Solution: compromise—improved labor-management relations
    2.1   Improved working conditions
    2.2   Progressive cost of living increase
    2.3   Job security after a probationary period
    2.4   Transfer of some workers to other jobs or departments
    2.5   Formation of a labor-management committee to hear grievances and prevent future strikes
3. Conclusion: end of strike

Fig. 31, An Example of Problem-solution Order—1.

Figure 32, following, is an example of problem-solution order as a development of the illustration of particular to general order on page 55.

DIAGNOSIS AND TREATMENT OF BOTULISM

1. Problem: sickness
    1.1 Effects: symptoms
        1.11 Double vision
        1.12 Drooping eyelids
        1.13 Difficulty in swallowing
        1.14 Difficulty in respiration
        1.15 Extreme muscular weakness
    1.2 Cause: botulism
2. Solution: treatment
    2.1 Pump out stomach
    2.2 Prescribe medication
        2.21 Dosage
        2.22 Time interval
        2.23 Bed rest
3. Conclusion: recovery

Fig. 32, An Example of Problem-solution Order—2.

Problem-solution reports are, of course, a standard of business and industry, but with a bit of imagination, you can apply this arrangement to many situations.

Comparison and contrast

Comparison and contrast enables you to compare two ideas, pieces of equipment, or methods of doing something, so that you can recommend one over the other. More than two things may, of course, be compared; in which case, preferences or alternatives are indicated, usually in the order of decreasing importance. The emphasis in comparison and contrast is on pointing out relationships, similarities and differences, and advantages and disadvantages.

At times, you may not wish to make a recommendation but leave the choice to your reader or your superior.

Figure 33, following, is an example of comparison and contrast in which two things can be compared directly, point by point.

GAS VS. ELECTRIC AIR CONDITIONING
FOR THE JOHN DOE COMPANY

1. Problem: choice of gas or electric air conditioning
2. Initial cost
   2.1 Gas
   2.2 Electricity
3. Installation
   3.1 Cost
       3.11 Gas
       3.12 Electricity
   3.2 Time
       3.21 Gas
       3.22 Electricity
4. Operation
   4.1 Cost
       4.11 Gas
       4.12 Electricity
   4.2 Efficiency
       4.21 Time to cool
           4.211 Gas
           4.212 Electricity
       4.22 Cooling capacity
           4.221 Gas
           4.222 Electricity
       4.23 Quietness of operation
           4.231 Gas
           4.232 Electricity
5. Maintenance
   5.1 Cost
       5.11 Gas
       5.12 Electricity
   5.2 Downtime
       5.21 Gas
       5.22 Electricity
6. Resale value
   6.1 Gas
   6.2 Electricity
7. Conclusions and recommendations

Fig. 33, An Example of Comparison and Contrast—1.

Naturally, some of the points will favor gas air conditioning, others will favor electric air conditioning, and still others will find them to be relatively equal; therefore, a conclusion will have to be made as to which is the better.

Figure 34, following, is an example of comparison and contrast in which the things compared are not directly comparable point by point. The advantages of one are not necessarily the disadvantages of the other and vice versa.

LOCATION OF A FACTORY FOR A GLASS COMPANY

I. In what city should a new glass factory be located—City A, City B, or City C?
  A. Requirements of the factory
  B. Sources of information
  C. Method of inquiry
II. City A
  A. Advantages
    1. ————
    2. ————
    3. ————
  B. Disadvantages
    1. ————
    2. ————
III. City B
  A. Advantages [list as above]
  B. Disadvantages [list as above]
IV. City C
  A. Advantages [list as above]
  B. Disadvantages [list as above]
  V. Conclusions and Recommendation

Fig. 34, An Example of Comparison and Contrast—2.

This outline violates topic outline form in that I is a complete sentence. In effect, it is a thesis statement.

Figure 35, following, is a more subtle treatment of the subject of Figure 34, as it permits a more direct comparison.

LOCATION OF A FACTORY FOR A GLASS COMPANY

I. Possible sites of a new glass factory—City A, City B, City C
  A. Requirements of the factory
  B. Sources of information
  C. Method of inquiry
II. City A
  A. Available land
    1. Location of the land
      a. With respect to means of transportation
      b. With respect to sources of raw materials
      c. With respect to available power
      d. With respect to available water
    2. Cost of land
  B. Building costs
  C. Available power and cost of power
  D. Available water and cost of water
  E. Available labor and prevailing wage scale of area
    1. Skilled
    2. Unskilled
    3. Union or non-union
  F. Taxes
  G. Available financing and cost of financing
  H. Climate and other considerations
  I. Local interest in the factory
  J. Problems
III. City B
  [Breakdown same as for City A.]
IV. City C
  [Breakdown same as for City A.]
  V. Conclusions and recommendations

Fig. 35, An Example of Comparison and Contrast—3.

Only two of the headings under City A in Figure 35 have been developed to any degree.

Comparison and contrast is an excellent pattern of development for many subjects. It is a particularly good presentation for persuasive speeches.

Known to unknown order

Known to unknown (or familiar to unfamiliar) order is similar to both problem-solution order and comparison and contrast. In known to unknown order, begin with what is known and work toward what is unknown: what the reader wants (or needs) to know—often the solution of a problem. Known to unknown order is the conventional order for the solution of mathematical problems.

Known to unknown order is related to comparison and contrast in that relationships can be drawn between things that are essentially dissimilar.

Figure 36, following, is an outline of an excerpt from one of the works of Oliver Wendell Holmes in which he discusses the chemical composition of the body with the lay reader in the familiar surroundings of the reader's breakfast table.

THE CHEMICAL COMPOSITION OF THE HUMAN BODY

I. Take a boiled egg "and instead of sacrificing it to a common appetite, devote it to the nobler hunger for knowledge."
   A. The effect of boiling an egg is to harden it.
   B. The substance which coagulates is the albumen, the raw material of the future chicken, "which may be coagulated into your breakfast by hot water, or into a chicken by the milder prolonged warmth of the mother's body."
II. "We can push the analysis further without any laboratory other than the breakfast-room."
   A. At the larger end of the egg is a small space containing air, oxygen and nitrogen.
   B. If a silver spoon is used to eat the egg, the spoon becomes discolored, the effect of sulphur, which gives a rotten egg its odor.
   C. If the contents of the egg are dried by heating them, water (hydrogen and oxygen) is driven off.
   D. If the scale that remains is burned, it forms animal charcoal (carbon).
   E. If this black crust is burned to ashes, chemical analysis will reveal various salts containing phosphorous, chlorine, potash, soda, magnesia, and iron.
   F. If the eggshell is burned, it becomes lime.
III. Following are the elements found in the egg: oxygen, hydrogen, carbon, nitrogen, sulphur, lime, iron, potash, soda, magnesia, phosphorus, chlorine.
   A. The six major constituents were determined by fireside chemistry.
   B. The other six are in minute quantities and had to be determined by chemical analysis.
   C. This egg, with its twelve elements, and nothing more, is capable of becoming a chicken with flesh, blood, and bones, a brain and nerves, and organs ready to function.
IV. "Just these same twelve elements, with the merest traces of two or three other substances, make up the human body."
   A. "All living things borrow their whole bodies from inanimate matter."
   B. Only a fraction of the substances found in nature are found in the most complex living body.

Fig. 36, An Example of Known to Unknown Order [Oliver Wendell Holmes, "Talk Concerning the Human Body and Its Management, by the Professor at the Breakfast Table," *Pages from an Old Volume of Life*, pp. 187–190. Houghton Mifflin Co. Boston: 1892].

Pro and con order

In pro and con order, present both sides of a controversial question and either draw a conclusion as to which is right (or better) or else leave it to the reader to draw his own conclusion from the evidence presented.

You can present the points of your argument in the order which will be most agreeable, pleasant, or acceptable to the reader if you wish to sway his opinion. For this reason, pro and con arrangement is often similar to psychological order. Normally, however, the points are presented in either the order of increasing or decreasing importance with respect to the two differing viewpoints.

Figure 37, following, is an example of pro and con order.

TRADING STAMPS

1. Do trading stamps raise or lower prices?
2. There are many reasons for giving and saving trading stamps.
    2.1   Trading stamps prove to be a remarkable promotion gimmick when first introduced by a business.
        2.11   Increased sales more than offset the cost of the stamps to department stores and supermarkets.
        2.12   They promote customer loyalty to the store.
    2.2   Premiums indirectly lower prices.
        2.21   They are worth approximately $3.00 per book to the customer in merchandise.
        2.22   They have a trade-in value of $2.00 per book in cash.
    2.3   They are a form of saving.
        2.31   Customers often save the books till they need something.
        2.32   They often use the books rather than cash for luxuries.
    2.4   Stamp companies claim that stores that stop giving stamps and lower prices, later raise their prices.
        2.41   The customer pays higher prices.
        2.42   But he no longer receives premiums.
    2.5   Stamps are now being given in many areas of business in which they were never given before, giving these businesses a competitive advantage from their use.
3. There are many reasons for abolishing the use of trading stamps.
    3.1   As more and more stores give stamps, the competitive advantage they at first offer disappears.
    3.2   They cost the stores 2 percent of gross sales.
        3.21   This cost is passed on to the customer, especially when the stamps no longer offer a competitive advantage.
        3.22   The price of the stamps remains fixed despite their loss of competitive advantage.

3.3 A survey has shown that only a small percentage of customers really want stamps.

3.4 Grocers have discovered that their customers shop around more than formerly, buying from several stores.

    3.41 Customers are more sophisticated now than in the past.

    3.42 They are more mobile, permitting them to shop around.

3.5 Grocers have started to fight competition with other means.

    3.51 They now offer greater product variety.

    3.52 They offer specials.

    3.53 They offer better parking facilities.

3.6 Both store owners and customers are becoming disenchanted with the stamp companies.

    3.61 Stamp companies have proliferated.

        3.611 Keeping so many different kinds of stamps has become a chore.

        3.612 Getting enough of one kind of stamps to get what one wants is increasingly difficult.

        3.613 It now takes more stamps to fill a book.

    3.62 Since many stamps are not redeemed, stamp companies are receiving more than 2 percent of gross sales.

4. Trading stamps are a mixed blessing.

    4.1 They lower prices in areas of competition and raise prices in areas of non-competition.

    4.2 They no longer offer a competitive advantage in areas in which they were originally given.

    4.3 They offer a competitive advantage in areas in which they have not been previously given.

    4.4 The discontinuance of trading stamps does not insure that prices will be reduced.

Fig. 37, An Example of Pro and Con Order.

Psychological order

In psychological order, present your subject in the order that will be most agreeable, pleasant, or acceptable to the reader. Since you appeal to the reader's tastes and personality, it is also called the order of acceptability. Psychological order is commonly used for organizing sales brochures, catalogs, and advertising. It is particularly effective for presenting arguments, for persuasion, and for explaining difficult subjects.

Psychological order is more effective when used for the overall pattern of organization than for the development of a single section. It requires a step-by-step development, a feeling of continuity. It is often combined with the order of increasing importance to give a sense of climax.

A mortician uses psychological order when he places an inexpensive coffin next to an expensive one and then compares the two coffins to the obvious disadvantage of the cheaper coffin in order to sell the one that is more expensive. Thus, psychological order is often combined with comparison and contrast and pro and con arrangement.

Since most readers are not swayed by logic alone, you may wish to supplement logical arguments with emotional appeals.

The danger of using psychological order is that it requires an intimate knowledge of the reader, a knowledge that you may not have. It is often objectionable because it lends itself to obvious flattery. Further, the text may be vague or difficult to follow because it violates natural or logical order.

Figure 38, following, is an example of psychological order which makes an emotional appeal to the reader.

LET'S BE THE BEST

I. Surely you want to be able to say that you are a graduate of the best university in America.
   A. If your school is recognized as the best, your degree will be more valuable.
      1. It will add dollars to your paycheck.
      2. It can assure faster promotions.
   B. If your school is recognized as the best, you will receive added prestige from being one of its graduates.
II. What can *you* do to insure that your university is the best?
   A. You can take a vital interest in its activities.
      1. You can join your local university club.
      2. You can join the alumni association.
      3. You can attend social functions, athletic events, and short courses on the campus.
   B. You can contribute directly to the university's improvement.
      1. You can write your state legislator in support of increasing the university's appropriation.
      2. You can interest your firm and your friends in contributing scholarships and other funds to the university.
      3. You can contribute directly to the university's Fund for Excellence.
III. Remember, *your university* cannot become the best without your help.
   A. Every graduate, every student, every faculty member, every staff member and administrator must do his share.
   B. *Without your help* your university can never become *the* best.

Fig. 38, An Example of Psychological Order.

Simple to complex order

In simple to complex order, start your discussion with the explanation of simple processes with which the reader is familiar, then build up to an explanation of a more complex process of which the simple processes are fundamental parts. For example, a salmon ladder that permits salmon to "climb" over a dam to make their way upriver to spawn is more like a staircase than a ladder. The riser of each step is a small dam that traps water, the tread of the stairs being water, not wood. The salmon ladder consists of a series of small dams, each one higher than the last, that rise step-by-step over the dam to the river beyond. The salmon leap from one tread to the next as they "step" over the dam.

At other times, you may explain simple procedures in order to make the operation of a related complex procedure more easily understood.

You may begin your discussion with easy-to-understand ideas (or processes) and then progress (point-by-point) to an explanation of a more complex idea (or process). This enables the reader to comprehend complex explanations by giving him the information in small, easily understood bits, usually in the order of their increasing difficulty, complexity, or importance. The explanation that was given earlier of the development of an outline from a scratch outline to a topic outline to a sentence outline is such a simple to complex development.

Simple to complex development is a common teaching technique.

Figure 39, following, is an example of simple to complex order in which simple processes are combined as parts of a more complex process.

HOW SALT IS OBTAINED FROM A SALT WELL

I. Three simple processes are combined in obtaining salt from salt wells.
    A. Salt combines with water to form a solution called brine.
    B. Water is released from a solution by heat.
    C. Loosely-packed solid particles can be separated by shaking them in a sieve.

II. Most of the salt produced in the United States comes from salt wells.
    A. A well is drilled into a salt deposit, in the same way that an oil or gas well is drilled.
    B. The salt well has a double pipe, one inside the other.
        1. Pure water is pumped down the outer pipe into the salt vein.
        2. The water combines with the salt to form brine.
        3. This brine is forced up the inner pipe and emptied into a brine tank at the surface.
    C. The brine is evaporated to salt by heating it in huge, low-pressure vacuum vats.
    D. A hot-air rotary drier removes the remaining water from the moist salt.
    E. The loosely-packed salt is separated by shaking it over fine screens.
    F. The salt is packed in sacks for shipment.

Fig. 39, An Example of Simple to Complex Order.

Order of need to know

The order of need to know is a rhetorical pattern commonly used in teaching: for lectures, textbooks, and reports on how-to-do something.

In the order of need to know, present information in the order in which the reader needs it to enable him to understand and use it most easily. For example, in a letter of inquiry, tell the reader the following information so that he can act upon your request quickly and effectively:

1. Who you are.

2. What you want.

3. Why you want it.

4. How you plan to use it.

5. What you can do for him in return.

The progress report given in Figure 40, following, is an example of the order of need to know in which section 2 is but one of a number of ways in which the subject could be developed.

A MODEL PROGRESS REPORT

1. Subject of the report
   - 1.1 Nature and scope of the problem
   - 1.2 Relation of this report to the previous reports
   - 1.3 Summary of progress to date and of period covered
   - 1.4 Conclusions, recommendations, and results to date
2. Work completed during this period
   - 2.1 Work unit completed
     - 2.11 Materials expended
     - 2.12 Equipment used
     - 2.13 Personnel employed
   - 2.2 Costs during the period
     - 2.21 Continuing expenses
     - 2.22 Special expenses
   - 2.3 Problems encountered
     - 2.31 Weather
     - 2.32 Accidents
     - 2.33 Equipment breakdown
     - 2.34 Material shortages
     - 2.35 Design problems

3. Plans for the future
    3.1 Next unit to be completed
    3.2 Proposals
4. Appendices
    4.1 Blueprints
    4.2 Tables

Fig. 40, An Example of the Order of Need to Know.

Traditional order

Some subjects are traditionally presented in a particular manner; therefore, you should follow the order conventionally used when writing on these subjects, as the reader will expect things to be presented in this order. If they are not, he may become angry or confused. Discussions of the federal government are traditionally presented under the headings "Executive," "Legislative," and "Judiciary" and taken up in that order.

Newspaper stories are traditionally written in the order of decreasing importance, so that if a story has to be cut, the editor can lop off the unimportant information at the end without having to make a value judgment of the information presented.

Petroleum engineering articles, papers, and reports traditionally begin with the conclusions and recommendations, followed by the summary, and then the body of the report in that order, as is illustrated in Figure 41, following.

DEEP DRILLING WITH CABLE TOOLS

1. Conclusions
2. Recommendations
3. Summary
4. Introduction
5. History and background of cable tool drilling
6. Equipment
    6.1 Derrick
    6.2 Rig wheels and power plant
    6.3 Cable and swivel socket
    6.4 String of tools and bit
7. Methods
8. Problems
9. References and bibliography

Fig. 41, An Example of Traditional Order.

Symbolical unity

At times, you may choose to use symbolical unity rather than some type of natural or logical order to organize your subject. Symbolical unity can be achieved through the use of imagination, mood, and symbol. Instead of using space (or geographical) order to organize a travel book, you might choose to present the flavor (or character) of a country by describing the changing countryside, climate, architecture, and the like along some major highway or river. U.S. Highway 66 was used as a unifying device for a television series to tie together a series of stories that were unrelated except for the protagonists who appeared in all of the episodes.

Authors have often used symbols to tie their works together. In *The Bridge of San Luis Rey*, Thornton Wilder tells the individual stories of a group of people who are killed when the bridge collapses. In *Grand Hotel*, Vicki Baum uses a hotel as a device to tie together a series of otherwise unrelated stories. In the play, *Outward Bound*, Sutton Vane uses a ship to achieve symbolical unity as does Katherine Anne Porter in her novel, *Ship of Fools*. And of course, two classic examples are Boccaccio's *Decameron* and Chaucer's *Canterbury Tales*, both of which use journeys (or pilgrimages) as a unifying device.

The tree is a common symbol for presenting subjects (such as language) that have a certain natural development. The cross is another commonly used device. Cattle brands, the signs of the zodiac, the ABC's—all can be used to give symbolical unity to loosely related ideas [see Fig. 28, p. 58]. The ABC's are a common device for arranging children's books, and combined with the symbol of Noah's Ark, they are often used for the organization of books about animals. The use of "Debits" and "Credits" as the basis of organizing an annual report is discussed under enumeration, pp. 57–59.

Still another example of symbolical unity is the story of the young soldier who was court martialed for playing cards in church. The soldier's defense was that each of the cards and the four suits reminded him of the Bible: the ace reminded him that there is but one God, the deuce reminded him of the two books of the Bible, the trey reminded him of the Holy Trinity, and so forth.

Figure 42, following, is an example of the use of books as a unifying symbol to present history [it is, of course, only a fragmentary list].

SOME BOOKS THAT HAVE SHAPED THE WORLD

1. *The Analects*—Confucious
   1.1 Sphere of influence ⎤
   1.2 Area of influence   ⎬ [following sections are developed alike]
   1.3 Period of influence ⎦
2. *Koran*—Mohammed
3. The Bible
4. *The Colloquies*—Erasmus
5. *The Prince*—Machiavelli
6. *L'Encyclopédie*—Diderot
7. *Commentaries on the Laws of England*—Blackstone
8. *Uncle Tom's Cabin*—Stowe
9. *On the Origin of Species by Means of Natural Selection*—Darwin
10. *Capital*—Marx
11. *A General Introduction to Psychology*—Freud
12. *Mein Kampf*—Hitler

Fig. 42, An Example of Symbolical Unity.

Topical order

In topical order (also referred to as the order of dominant impression), present your subject according to its major topics. Instead of presenting history in strict chronological sequence, you can present it from the point of view of important events or individuals.

Topical order is commonly combined with time order, history being presented largely in time order with various parts being arranged according to topical order to achieve a desired emphasis. As mentioned above, topical order can take precedence over time order—for example, in a collection of biographical sketches.

Figure 42 is an example of topical order as well as an example of symbolical unity.

Figure 43, following, is an example of topical order combined with time order. All sections are developed like the first, and only the first three presidents are listed.

THE PRESIDENTS AND THEIR EFFECT ON HISTORY

1. George Washington
   1.1 Period of service
   1.2 Qualities of leadership
   1.3 Events during his term of office
      1.31 In government and foreign affairs
      1.32 In science and invention
      1.33 In transportation and commerce
      1.34 In industry
      1.35 In agriculture
      1.36 In literature and the arts
2. John Adams
3. Thomas Jefferson

Fig. 43, An Example of Topical Order.

Which of the foregoing twenty-two patterns of organization you use to develop your speech or paper will largely determine its clarity, completeness, and effectiveness; therefore, you should learn to distinguish between closely related and overlapping types of arrangement in order to make the best possible choice.

5

Development

The major divisions of a conventionally organized paper or speech are the introduction, the body, and the conclusion. These major divisions should be developed in detail with explanation, examples, and illustrations so that your reader or audience can understand and use the information presented.

The Introduction

The introduction of your paper "introduces" your subject to your reader and gives him the necessary background to understand the information presented in the body. The introduction normally includes one or more of the elements listed in Figure 44, following.

A CHECK LIST FOR EVALUATING INTRODUCTIONS

1. A statement of the subject of your paper.
2. A statement of its purpose.
3. A statement of for whom it is intended.
4. A history and background of the problem.
5. A definition of terms.
6. A distinction between primary and secondary problems.
7. A distinction between what is known and what needs to be known.
8. A review of the literature in the field.
9. A discussion of similar studies.
10. A statement of the plan of development.
11. A summary of the paper.
12. A list of conclusions that can be drawn.
13. A list of recommendations that can be made.
14. Any other information necessary to enable the reader to understand the body of the paper.

Fig. 44, A Check List for Evaluating Introductions.

Present a direct statement of the subject (or problem) at the outset. Too much writing fails because the writer does not make a clear statement of what his paper is about, either quickly enough or at all.

Normally, the introduction gives a breakdown of the subject into its component parts (in the order in which they are presented in the body) to give the reader an understanding of the plan of development so that he will know what is to follow. If more information is needed to increase the reader's understanding, a summary (referred to as an introductory-summary) is given. This enables the reader to be in the position of a person working a jigsaw puzzle after first having seen a picture of how the puzzle will look once it is completed, as the introductory-summary "pictures" the paper in miniature.

Conclusions and recommendations are given in the introduction for the same reason: to give the reader as much information at the outset as possible to make it easier for him to understand the information presented in the body. One of the major reasons for poor writing is the writer's failure to give the reader sufficient information at the start, either through carelessness or assuming too much knowledge on the part of the reader.

The Body

The body of the paper contains the development of the subject: the facts, definitions, description, examples, statistics, and opinions that explain, illustrate, or prove your thesis.

Your paper should be developed in single units called paragraphs. Paragraphs are commonly of two types: either (1) a list of details which add up to a total impression given in a summary sentence at or near the end of the paragraph; or (2) a topic sentence followed by specific details that support or illustrate it. These two basic patterns of paragraph development follow the order of particular to general and general to particular. Paragraphs can be developed using other types of arrangement used for the paper as a whole—comparison and contrast, cause to effect, increasing importance, and the like.

Explanation

Explanation is the most common and easiest to use method of development. It is used to answer the basic questions *who, what, where, when, why,* and *how.*

Explanation should be simple, brief, clear, and accurate. It can include definition, description, enumeration, interpretation, and qualification.

It is usually not complete in itself; therefore, it should be used in combination with one or more of the other types of development.

Comparison, contrast, and analogy

Comparison and contrast provide not only an effective pattern for arrangement but also for development. Comparison and contrast are used to point out the similarities and differences between two or more ideas or things to enable you to discuss them more easily and effectively. Although comparison implies contrast, many people prefer to use *comparison* to mean *likeness* and *contrast* to mean *difference*.

You can achieve clarity in your writing by comparing the unfamiliar to the familiar (what the reader does not know to what he can be assumed to know).

Analogy permits the comparison of two things that are basically dissimilar, but which are alike in certain respects. A building can be said to be L-shaped or shaped like a capital H, for example. Comparison and contrast (as well as analogy) lend themselves to the use of simile and metaphor. Erosion on a farm can be said to be "like the Grand Canyon in miniature." This simile (or comparison) shows both likeness ("like the Grand Canyon") and difference ("in miniature").

Developed examples

Developed examples (or anecdotes) are brief stories that make a point and illustrate abstract ideas to help the reader grasp and remember them. They are often witty or humorous.

Developed examples are of two types, factual and hypothetical. Factual examples, since they tell what *has* happened, convey a feeling of verisimilitude, whereas hypothetical examples, which tell what *could* happen, tend to be less convincing since they are often so obviously made up. Therefore, it is better to tell a hypothetical illustration as if it happened to you or to someone else, giving the people and places names, rather than saying, "a man" or "three boys."

Specific instances

Specific instances are statements of fact that illustrate or support a point. They need little or no explanation, being largely complete in themselves. They are frequently used for presenting general statistics, such as "Most accidents occur on east-west streets, either early in the morning or late in the afternoon, when drivers are facing the sun."

Statistics

Statistics are one of the most persuasive means of developing a point. They permit you to present a mass of information quickly, usually in tabular form, which permits the reader to compare them to see their relationships. You should round off numbers when possible, saying "approximately 300," rather than 298, when the specific number is not important, since rounding off numbers makes them easier to grasp and remember.

Testimony of authorities

The testimony of authorities is used when facts are not available. When the reader may be expected to question your ideas, support them with the "educated guesses" of authorities in the field.

Do not use an authority in one field as an expert witness in another field unless he can be shown to be expert in both fields. If the reader cannot be expected to recognize the authority's name, be sure to qualify who the authority is and how he is qualified by education and experience to testify on the subject.

Restatement

Restatement (or repetition) is the weakest type of development, but it does serve a purpose. Its strength lies in the fact that repetition helps the reader to grasp and remember a point under discussion. It is most effective when the point is repeated each time in different words and from a different viewpoint—but shifting your viewpoint should be done with care to avoid confusion.

The Conclusion

The conclusion of your paper should bring your discussion to a measured stop, not an abrupt halt that leaves the reader dangling in air. It should consist of one or a combination of the elements in Figure 45, following.

A CHECK LIST FOR EVALUATING CONCLUSIONS

1. A brief concluding statement.
2. A restatement of the thesis.
3. A summary of the main points.
4. A question to be answered by the reader or by further study.
5. A suggestion that the problem be given further study.
6. An appeal for action on the part of the reader.
7. A conclusion or a series of conclusions.
8. A recommendation or a series of recommendations.

Fig. 45, A Check List for Evaluating Conclusions.

The conclusion to a paper commonly consists of a brief summary of the subject or your conclusions and recommendations with respect to it. Conclusions and recommendations should be positive rather than negative statements for clarity and emphasis. If you give both general and specific conclusions and recommendations, the general conclusions and recommendations should precede the specific. Conclusions and recommendations are often numbered and listed separately for ready reference.

If the conclusion consists only of a brief statement which says, in effect, "This is the end," it is ordinarily tacked onto the body of the paper rather than set off under a separate heading.

A Final Word

When you are ready to begin writing, arrange your notes in outline order, so that they can be easily used in conjunction with your outline. Wear comfortable clothing. Work at a desk where you have proper light and sufficient room so that you can have all of the necessary tools for writing and reference close at hand.

If writing is to take place over a prolonged period of time, as when writing a long report, set up habits (or patterns) of work, so that you can get into the rhythm of writing each day with a minimum of wasted time and effort.

Remember that what you write is only as good as the ideas and information that go into the writing. A detailed, logically developed outline is the best way to insure that your writing will contain worthwhile ideas and information.